NEHRU

Also by Shashi Tharoor

Reasons of State

India: From Midnight to the Millennium

The Five Dollar Smile and Other Stories

The Great Indian Novel

Show Business

Riot

NEHRU

THE INVENTION OF INDIA

SHASHI THAROOR

Arcade Publishing • New York

FIRST EDITION

Though the author is a senior official of the United Nations, none of the opinions expressed in this book are to be construed as those of the organization or of the author in his official capacity.

Library of Congress Cataloging-in-Publication Data

Tharoor, Shashi, 1956–
Nehru: the invention of India / by Shashi Tharoor.
p. cm.
ISBN 1-55970-697-X
1. Nehru, Jawaharlal, 1889–1964. 2. Prime ministers—India—Biography. 3. India—Politics and government.

DS481.N35N38 2003
954.04'2'092—dc22 2003058274

Published in the United States by Arcade Publishing, Inc., New York
Distributed by AOL Time Warner Book Group

10 9 8 7 6 5 4 3 2 1

Designed by API

EB

PRINTED IN THE UNITED STATES OF AMERICA

To Kofi Annan,
who, as a young man in Ghana,
admired Nehru,
this book is dedicated
with respect and affection

Contents

Preface

For the first seventeen years of India's independence, the paradox-ridden Jawaharlal Nehru — a moody, idealist intellectual who felt an almost mystical empathy with the toiling peasant masses; an aristocrat, accustomed to privilege, who had passionate socialist convictions; an Anglicized product of Harrow and Cambridge who spent almost ten years in British jails; an agnostic radical who became an unlikely protégé of the saintly Mahatma Gandhi — *was* India. Upon the Mahatma's assassination, Nehru became the keeper of the national flame, the most visible embodiment of India's struggle for freedom. Incorruptible, visionary, ecumenical, a politician above politics, Nehru's stature was so great that the country he led seemed inconceivable without him. A year before his death a leading American journalist published a book entitled *After Nehru, Who?* The unspoken question around the world was: "after Nehru, what?"

Today, nearly four decades after his death, we have something of an answer to the latter question. As an India still seemingly clad in the trappings of Nehruvianism steps out into the twenty-first century, little of Jawaharlal Nehru's legacy appears intact. India has moved away from much of it, and so (in different ways) has the rest of the developing world for which Nehruvianism once spoke. As India nears the completion of the sixth decade of its independence from the British Raj, a transformation — still incomplete — has taken place that, in its essentials, has changed the basic Nehruvian assumptions of postcolonial nationhood.

In this short biography, I have sought to examine this great figure of twentieth-century nationalism from the vantage point of the beginning of the twenty-first. Jawaharlal Nehru's life is a fascinating story in its own right, and I have tried to tell it whole, because the privileged child, the unremarkable youth, the posturing young nationalist, and the heroic fighter for independence are all inextricable from the unchallengeable prime minister and revered global statesman. A concluding chapter critically analyzes the principal pillars of Nehru's legacy to India — democratic institution-building, staunch pan-Indian secularism, socialist economics at home, and a foreign policy of nonalignment — all of which were integral to a vision of Indianness that is fundamentally contested today.

Nehru: The Invention of India is not a scholarly work; it is based on no new research into previously undiscovered archives; it is not footnoted, though a Note on Sources and a Select Bibliography will guide the curious toward further reading. It is, instead, a reinterpretation — both of an extraordinary life and career and of the inheritance it left behind for every Indian. The very term "Indian" was imbued with such meaning by Nehru that it is impossible to use it without acknowledging a debt: our passports incarnate his ideals. Where those ideals came from, whether they were brought to fulfillment by their own progenitor, and to what degree they remain viable today are among the themes of this book. I started it as divided between admiration and criticism as I finished it; but the more I delved into Nehru's life, it was the admiration which deepened.

Jawaharlal Nehru's impact on India is too great not to be reexamined periodically. As an Indian writer, I am conscious that his legacy is ours, whether we agree with everything he stood for or not. What India is today, both for good and for ill, we owe in great measure to one man. This is his story.

A Note on Indian Political Movements

This book mentions a number of Indian political parties and movements of importance to understanding Jawaharlal Nehru's life and times and appreciating his legacy.

The **Indian National Congress** was founded in 1885 by a liberal Scotsman, Allan Octavian Hume, to provide a forum for the articulation of an Indian viewpoint on issues of the country's governance and political development. The Congress evolved into the country's premier political party (whose annual sessions, in different venues around India, attracted ever-greater attendance and attention). Its leadership was initially drawn from the educated professional classes, and its presidents, who were elected annually, belonged to various faiths, with Hindus, Muslims, Christians, and Parsis among the first two dozen presidents. Around the cusp of the century a schism developed within the Congress between the Extremists, led by Tilak, and the Moderates, led by Gokhale — the former seeking more radical action to overthrow the British, the latter pursuing their goals through constitutional means while seeking fundamental reforms leading to self-government. This schism ended around the time of the First World War.

The advent of Mahatma Gandhi, who returned to India from a long sojourn in South Africa in 1916, transformed the Congress from an elite debating society passing largely ineffectual resolutions into a mass movement for complete independence. In order to engage the Muslim masses and to promote Hindu-Muslim unity, Gandhi committed the party to supporting the **Khilafat** movement, which organized anti-British demonstrations around India clamoring for the restoration of the Caliphate in the defeated Ottoman Turkey. The victory of the secular republican Kemal Ataturk in the Turkish civil war rendered that cause otiose, but the campaign demonstrated both the potential and the limitations of popular mobilization cutting across communal lines. During the 1920s the major division in the Congress Party was between those advocating civil disobedience and noncooperation with the British and those who, calling themselves **Swarajists**, contested elections for seats in the institutions of limited self-governance allowed by the British. By the turn of the decade, though, both groups had reunited under Mahatma Gandhi's leadership to demand full independence (though many were prepared to settle for Dominion status within the British Empire). The principal differences within the Congress through the 1930s were between the radical socialists and the more conservative party elders. As the book explains, Jawaharlal Nehru had a foot in both camps.

Outside the Congress, a number of minor parties advanced various particularist interests, of which the main group mentioned in this book is the **Liberal Party**, led by Sir Tej Bahadur Sapru, which sought to work with the British to progressively expand Indian self-rule. The Liberals had little popular support and sought no mass base, but the British accorded them attention out of proportion to their political importance.

In the meantime, a far more fundamental challenge developed within the nationalist movement, this time not on ideological or tactical lines but on communal ones. The **All-India Muslim League** was founded in 1906 after a deputation of Muslim notables called on the viceroy to affirm their loyalty to British rule and seek the authorities' support for Muslim interests. For a long time the League was not seen as a viable alternative to the Congress, and indeed many of its leaders enjoyed membership in both bodies. Up until the late 1920s it is possible to find the same names presiding over different sessions of the Congress and the League. Serious differences arose in the course of the Gandhian success at mass mobilization, leading the League, under Mohammed Ali Jinnah, principally out of fear of the consequences of "majority rule" (which they saw as likely to permit Hindu domination), to develop an increasingly separatist platform. While the Congress claimed throughout to represent Indians of all faiths, and continued to have important

Muslim leaders (notably Maulana Abul Kalam Azad, its president from 1940 to 1946, and Khan Abdul Ghaffar Khan, the "Frontier Gandhi"), the League increasingly asserted that it alone spoke for India's Muslims. Though various regional parties sought to transcend the Congress-League divide by including members of all communities on nonsectarian platforms — notably the **Unionist Party** in Punjab, which advanced agrarian interests, and the **Krishak Mazdoor Praja Party** (Farmers, Workers, and Tenants Party) in Bengal — the League eventually triumphed in its aspirations. This book describes the evolution of the chasm between the Congress and the League and its ultimate conclusion — the partition of the country into two states, India and Pakistan, when the British left in 1947.

One other political movement deserves mention. Hindutva, literally "Hinduness," is the cause advanced by Hindu zealots who harken back to atavistic pride in India's Hindu heritage and seek to replace the country's secular institutions with a Hindu state. Their forebears during the nationalist struggle were the **Hindu Mahasabha**, a party advancing Hindu communal interests neglected by the secular Congress, and the **Rashtriya Swayamsevak Sangh** (RSS), or National Volunteer Corps, modeled on the Italian Brown Shirts. Neither found much traction within the Congress, and the Hindu Mahasabha faded away, but the creation of Pakistan and the terrible communal bloodletting that accompanied partition provided Hindu zealots new sources of support. The **Bharatiya Jana Sangh**, or Indian People's Party, was founded after independence as the principal vehicle for their political aspirations. The Sangh merged into the short-lived omnibus party, the Janata, in 1977, and reemerged in 1980 as the **Bharatiya Janata Party**, or BJP. Today the principal votaries of Hindutva are a "family" of organizations collectively known as the Sangh Parivar, including the RSS, the Vishwa Hindu Parishad (World Hindu Council), the Bajrang Dal, and a large portion of the Bharatiya Janata Party, which since 1998 heads a coalition government in New Delhi.

THE NEHRU FAMILY TREE: FIVE GENERATIONS

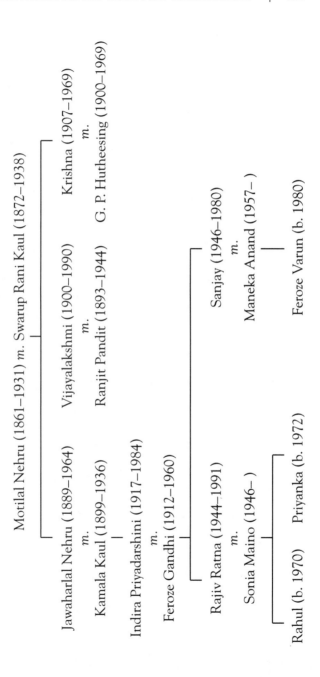

Motilal Nehru (1861–1931) *m.* Swarup Rani Kaul (1872–1938)

- Jawaharlal Nehru (1889–1964) *m.* Kamala Kaul (1899–1936)
  - Indira Priyadarshini (1917–1984) *m.* Feroze Gandhi (1912–1960)
    - Rajiv Ratna (1944–1991) *m.* Sonia Maino (1946–)
      - Rahul (b. 1970)
      - Priyanka (b. 1972)
    - Sanjay (1946–1980) *m.* Maneka Anand (1957–)
      - Feroze Varun (b. 1980)
- Vijayalakshmi (1900–1990) *m.* Ranjit Pandit (1893–1944)
- Krishna (1907–1969) *m.* G. P. Hutheesing (1900–1969)

NEHRU

1

"With Little to Commend Me": 1889–1912

In January 1889, or so the story goes, Motilal Nehru, a twenty-seven-year-old lawyer from the north Indian city of Allahabad, traveled to Rishikesh, a town holy to Hindus, up in the foothills of the Himalayas on the banks of the sacred river Ganga (Ganges). Motilal was weighed down by personal tragedy. Married as a teenager, in keeping with custom, he had soon been widowed, losing both his wife and his firstborn son in childbirth. In due course he had married again, an exquisitely beautiful woman named Swarup Rani Kaul. She soon blessed him with another son — but the boy died in infancy. Motilal's own brother Nandlal Nehru then died at the age of forty-two, leaving to Motilal the care of his widow and seven children. The burden was one he was prepared to bear, but he desperately sought the compensatory joy of a son of his own. This, it seemed, was not to be.

Motilal and his two companions, young Brahmins of his acquaintance, visited a famous yogi renowned for the austerities he practiced while living in a tree. In the bitter cold of winter, the yogi undertook various penances, which, it was said, gave him great powers. One of the travelers, Pandit Madan Mohan Malaviya, informed the yogi that Motilal's greatest desire in life was to have a son. The yogi asked Motilal to step forward, looked at him long and hard, and shook his head sadly: "You," he declared, "will not have a son. It is not in your destiny."

As a despairing Motilal stood crestfallen before him, the other man, the learned Pandit Din Dayal Shastri, argued respectfully with the yogi. The ancient Hindu shastras, he said, made it clear that there was nothing irreversible about such a fate; a great karmayogi like him could simply grant the unfortunate man a boon. Thus challenged, the yogi looked at the young men before him, and finally sighed. He reached into his brass pitcher and sprinkled water from it three times upon the would-be father. Motilal began to express his gratitude, but the yogi cut him short. "By doing this," the yogi breathed, "I have sacrificed all the benefits of all the austerities I have conducted over many generations."

The next day, as legend has it, the yogi passed away.

Ten months later, at 11:30 P.M. on November 14, 1889, Motilal Nehru's wife, Swarup Rani, gave birth to a healthy baby boy. He was named Jawaharlal ("precious jewel"), and he would grow up to be one of the most remarkable men of the twentieth century.

Jawaharlal Nehru himself always disavowed the story as apocryphal, though it was attributed by many to two of the protagonists themselves — Motilal and Malaviya. Since neither left a firsthand account of the episode, the veracity of the tale can never be satisfactorily determined. Great men are often ascribed remarkable beginnings, and at the peak of Jawaharlal Nehru's career there were many willing to promote a supernatural explanation for his greatness. His father, certainly, saw him from a very early age as a child of destiny, one made for extraordinary success; but as a rationalist himself, Motilal is unlikely to have based his faith in his son on a yogi's blessing.

The child himself was slow to reveal any signs of potential greatness. He was the kind of student usually referred to as "indifferent." He also luxuriated in the pampering of parents whose affluence grew with the mounting success of Motilal Nehru's legal career. In a pattern well-known in traditional Indian life, where wives received very little companionship from their husbands and transferred their emotional attentions to their sons instead, Jawaharlal was smothered with affection by his mother, in whom he saw "Dresden china perfection." Years later he would begin his autobiography with the confession: "An only son of prosperous parents is apt to be spoilt, especially so in India. And when that son happens to have been an only child for the first eleven years of his existence, there is little hope for him to escape this spoiling."

The young Jawaharlal Nehru's mind was shaped by two sets of parental influences that he never saw as contradictory — the traditional Hinduism of his mother and the other womenfolk of the Nehru household, and the modernist, secular cosmopolitanism of his father. The women (especially Swarup's widowed sister Rajvati) told him tales from Hindu mythology, took him regularly to temples, and immersed him for baths in the holy river Ganga. Motilal, on the other hand, though he never disavowed the Hindu faith into which he was born, refused to undergo a "purification ceremony" in order to atone formally for having "crossed the black water" by traveling abroad, and in 1899 was formally excommunicated by the high-caste Hindu elders of Allahabad for his intransigence. The taint lingered, and Motilal's family was socially boycotted by some of the purists, but the Nehrus typically rose above the ostracism through their own worldly success.

The Nehrus were Kashmiri Pandits, scions of a community of Brahmins from the northernmost reaches of the subcontinent who had made new lives for themselves across northern and central India since at least the eighteenth century. Kashmir itself had been largely converted to Islam in the sixteenth and seventeenth centuries, but Kashmiri Muslims followed a syncretic version of the faith imbued with the gentle mysticism of Sufi preachers, and coexisted in harmony with their Hindu neighbors. Though the Pandits left Kashmir in significant numbers, they did so not as refugees fleeing Muslim depredation, but as educated and professionally skilled migrants in quest of better opportunities. Though the Kashmiri Pandits were as clannish a community as any in India — conscious that their origins, their modest numbers, their high social standing, and their pale, fine-featured looks all made them special — they were proud of their pan-Indian outlook. They had, after all, left their original homes behind in the place they still called their "motherland," Kashmir; they had thrived in a state where Muslims outnumbered them thirteen to one; they had no history of casteist quarrels, since the non-Brahmin castes of Kashmir, and several of the Brahmins, had converted to Islam; they were comfortable with Muslim culture, with the Persian language, and even with the eating of meat (which most Indian Brahmins other than Kashmiris and Bengalis abjured). Secure in themselves and at ease with others, Kashmiri Pandits inclined instinctively toward the cosmopolitan. It was no accident, for instance, that Motilal's chief household retainer was a Muslim, Munshi Mubarak Ali. Jawaharlal learned a great deal from him: "With his fine grey beard he seemed to my young eyes very ancient and full of old-time lore, and I used to snuggle up to him and listen, wide-eyed, by the hour to his innumerable stories."

The family's original name was Kaul. Jawaharlal Nehru's ancestor Raj Kaul settled in Mughal Delhi in the eighteenth century and, perhaps because there were other Kauls of prominence in the city, assumed the hyphenated name of Kaul-Nehru, the suffix indicating the family's residence on the edge of a canal, or *nehar* in Urdu. (It is also possible the name came from the village of Naru in the Badgam district of Kashmir, but this has never been conclusively established.) The Kaul-Nehrus moved to Agra in the mid-nineteenth century, where the compound form soon disappeared. It was simply as a Nehru that Motilal made his name at the Allahabad bar.

Along with the name and the money that came with

his success as a lawyer, Motilal acquired the trappings of a Victorian gentleman of means — an elegant house (named Anand Bhavan, or "Abode of Bliss") in a desirable residential area, with mostly British neighbors; a fancy carriage; a stable of Arabian steeds; and a wardrobe full of English suits, many tailored in Savile Row. Jawaharlal grew up surrounded by every imaginable creature comfort. Not only did he have electricity and running water in the house (both unheard-of luxuries for most of his compatriots), but the family home was equipped with such unusual perquisites as a private swimming pool and a tennis court, and his father ordered the latest toys for him from England, including the newly invented tricycle and bicycle. (Motilal himself owned Allahabad's first car, imported in 1904.) Jawaharlal enjoyed lavish birthday parties, holidays in Kashmir, a plenitude of clothes — a classic Little Lord Fauntleroy upbringing.

The allusion is not too far-fetched. There is a studio photograph of Jawaharlal aged five in 1894, attired in a navy blue sailor suit, his hair neatly combed under a high stiff collar, his little hands firmly grasped between his knees, while the paterfamilias looms above, left arm cocked at his side, gold watch-chain at his waist, surveying the world with gimlet eyes above his handlebar moustache. Swarup Rani Nehru, seated to the side in an elaborate sari, seems almost marginal to this striking tableau of bourgeois Victorian male authority. (There is another photograph of mother and son: this time, Jawaharlal is in Indian clothes, and Motilal is absent.)

It was at about this time that an episode occurred that Jawaharlal would recall for decades afterward. His

father had two fine pens in an inkstand atop his mahogany desk, which caught the young boy's eye. Thinking that Motilal "could not require both at the same time," Jawaharlal took one for his lessons. When Motilal found it missing, a furious search ensued. The frightened boy first hid the pen and then himself, but he was soon discovered by servants and turned in to his enraged father. What ensued was, in Jawaharlal's recollection, "a tremendous thrashing. Almost blind with pain and mortification at my disgrace, I rushed to my mother, and for several days various creams and ointments were applied to my aching and quivering little body." He learned much from this experience: not to cross his father, not to lay claim to what was not his, not to conceal evidence of his own wrongdoing, if ever he were to do wrong — and never to assume he could simply "get away with it." It was a lesson which had much to do with the sense of responsibility that became a defining Nehru characteristic.

Motilal and Jawaharlal remained the only male Nehrus in the immediate family. A sister, Sarup Kumari (who would one day be known to the world as the glamorous Vijayalakshmi Pandit, the first woman president of the United Nations General Assembly), was born on August 18, 1900. On Jawaharlal's sixteenth birthday, another ill-fated boy was born; he died within a month, the third of Motilal's four sons to fail to outlive his infancy. Two years later, on November 2, 1907, the last of Jawaharlal Nehru's siblings, another sister, Krishna, emerged. The older of the two girls was nicknamed "Nanhi," or "little one" in Hindi, the younger "Beti," or "daughter." Their English governesses quickly transmuted these diminutives to "Nan" and "Betty" respectively, and it was the Anglicized versions of the nicknames that stuck, not the Hindi ones.

Indeed, Jawaharlal Nehru's sailor suit in that early photograph was not just for posing. It embodied the Westernization of his early upbringing; he had two British governesses at home, and from 1901 to 1904 a private tutor, the Irish-French Ferdinand T. Brooks, who taught him English poetry and the rudiments of science from a lab he rigged up at home, and instilled in him a lifelong love of reading (the young Jawaharlal devoured Scott and Dickens, Conan Doyle and Twain). Motilal also engaged an eminent Sanskrit tutor, who reportedly had little success with his Anglophone charge. But Brooks, a follower of theosophy — a conflation of Hindu doctrines and Christian ethics that reached its peak of popularity in the last decades of the nineteenth century — obliged Jawaharlal to read the Upanishads and the Bhagavad Gita in English translation, and the young Nehru even briefly went through a formal conversion to theosophy at age thirteen (though this was soon forgotten by all concerned, including the convert himself). The woman who initiated Jawaharlal into theosophy, Annie Besant, a silver-tongued Englishwoman who had joined the struggle for Indian "home rule," would remain a powerful influence in the years to come.

Meanwhile, the boy was doted on by his increasingly unwell mother, who superstitiously went to inordinate lengths to protect him from the "evil eye" — that malefic gaze, born of envy or even excessive admiration, which many Hindus believe brings disaster in its wake.

She would admonish anyone who commented on his looks, his growth, his talents, or even his appetite (it is said she would give him a private snack before dinner so that he would not eat too hungrily before others and invite comment). Jawaharlal was frequently subjected to ritual attempts to ward off possible afflictions, including the placing of a black dot on the forehead to repel the evil eye, which of course was rubbed off before the lad posed for the studio photographs of the family with Motilal.

Motilal had little time for such distractions as religion or custom; the hereafter concerned him less than the here and now. A freethinking rationalist, he saw in Western science and English reasoning, rather than in Hindu religion or ritual, the real hope of progress for India. He sometimes took this conviction too far: at one point in the 1890s he decreed that no language other than English would be spoken at his home, having forgotten that none of the female Nehrus had been taught any English. Inevitably, when Jawaharlal was just fifteen, his father enrolled him at the prestigious British public school, Harrow.

By an intriguing coincidence, some fifteen years earlier the school had educated (and sent on to Sandhurst) a young man called Winston Spencer Churchill, who after stints in the colonies was already embarking upon a prodigious career in British public life. The two Harrovians would come to have diametrically opposed views of India — dismissive on Churchill's part, proudly nationalist on Nehru's. "India," Churchill once barked, "is not a country or a nation. . . . It is merely a geographical expression. It is no more a single country than the Equator." A more liberal-minded Harrovian of the previous century, Sir William Jones, had founded the Asiatic Society of Bengal in 1784, translated many Sanskrit classics, and greatly advanced Western appreciation of Indian culture and philosophy. But ironically, it was Churchill's view of India that would one day make Jawaharlal Nehru's "invention of India" necessary. "Such unity of sentiment as exists in India," Churchill wrote, "arises entirely through the centralized British Government of India as expressed in the only common language of India — English." Jawaharlal Nehru, as the product of the same elite British school as Churchill, would use that education and the English language to complete what he called "the discovery of India" and assert its right to be free of Churchill's government.

There are a couple of photographs of Jawaharlal Nehru at Harrow, aged about seventeen, one of him sulky in the khaki uniform of the Harrow School Cadet Corps, his cheek bisected by the chinstrap of a faintly absurd helmet, the other in more conventional pose (dark suit, left hand in pocket, boater in right, a somewhat abstracted gaze just avoiding the camera's lens). Neither photo reveals the moustache he sometimes maintained out of deference to his hirsute father (who told his son bluntly that his clean-shaven face made him "look like a fool"). But they suggest a well-adjusted Harrovian, comfortable enough in himself, and to that extent the photographs do not mislead. Jawaharlal did well at school, impressing his teachers with his "industry and ability," his willingness to prepare for his classes, and the quality of his "English subjects" (though his French and Latin were never quite up to the mark). Harrow confirmed what would become a lifelong faith in physical fitness; "Joe" Nehru played football and cricket (though neither particularly well), ran fairly seriously (he competed in the school's half-mile and mile racing events and the cross-country steeplechase, which testifies to a level of fitness and stamina that his slight build does not suggest), and was often found ice-skating or performing calisthenics in the gymnasium. He also took an avid interest in the Officers' Training Corps.

Harrow was an experience Nehru always cherished, though contemporaries interviewed by his preeminent biographer, Sarvepalli Gopal, largely remembered him as "average" and "undistinguished." Nehru himself described his Harrovian experience as a happy one, which he had wept at having to leave behind. Not enough credit is given — not even by Gopal — to young Jawaharlal's remarkable ability, after a cloistered upbringing in Allahabad, to adjust to a new country, a new climate, and the rigors of a new school, and to do well enough there so that, in prison three decades later, he would find solace in inserting pictures of Harrow into his diaries.

It was during Jawaharlal's years at Harrow that Indian nationalist politics, hitherto a largely genteel affair, took a dramatic turn with the mass agitation against the British decision in 1905 to partition the province of Bengal. The Indian National Congress, which had been founded in 1885, four years before Jawaharlal's birth, by a liberal Scotsman, Allan Octavian Hume, was coming of age. The first Congress was attended by seventy-two

Indian delegates. Three years later, Motilal had been one of fourteen hundred delegates at the Allahabad Congress of 1888, but had not remained directly active in the cause. Jawaharlal, though, took a keen interest in news of Indian political developments. Letters from his father, and clippings from Indian newspapers Motilal sent him, kept the adolescent apprised of the Swadeshi movement (which urged Indians to reject British goods and use only items of Indian manufacture), the division within the Indian National Congress between the "Extremists" and the "Moderates" (broadly, the agitationists, led by the lecturer, journalist, and historian Bal Gangadhar Tilak, and the constitutionalists, led by the teacher and social reformer Gopal Krishna Gokhale), and the eventual British capitulation on the issue of Bengal's partition (which was, under popular pressure, duly reversed). Jawaharlal expressed admiration for the nationalism of Tilak and the Extremists, criticizing his father for being "immoderately moderate." Years later he recognized that his father's objections to the Extremists were based less on a dislike of their methods than on the Hindu nationalism they expressed, at odds with Motilal's own secular cosmopolitanism.

The radical streak in Jawaharlal Nehru began to show from the moment of his arrival in England, when news of the Japanese naval triumph over Russia at Tsushima in 1905 thrilled him with the realization that a great European power could be defeated by an Asian nation. A later visit to Ireland also revealed to Jawaharlal the force of nationalist agitation, with the Sinn Fein movement and Irish calls for a boycott of British goods reinforcing his Extremist sympathies. He also read widely, developing a great admiration for the works of George Bernard Shaw, and finding in the books of some British writers of the period, notably William Morris and Meredith Townsend, persuasive arguments against both capitalism and imperialism that seemed to predict the inevitable decline of the British Raj in India. A school prize was Trevelyan's biography of Garibaldi, which inspired in the young Nehru "visions of similar deeds in India."

In October 1907 Jawaharlal Nehru entered Trinity College, Cambridge, having passed the entrance examinations somewhat earlier than either his father or his headmaster thought he should have attempted them. By all accounts his does not appear to have been a particularly active or distinguished undergraduate life. He studied chemistry, geology, and physics (later swapping physics for botany) and graduated with a mediocre second-class degree. Though in later years he was to be identified with the Fabian Socialism that had already begun to flourish in Cambridge intellectual circles, there is no evidence of his having had anything to do with the Fabian Society at the university. He joined various debating societies but almost never spoke; nor was he an exceptionally prominent member of the Indian Majlis, the Indian students' group, which held its own public meetings and debates. To some degree this was a reflection of a shyness in public that he would have to work hard to overcome in later life. To an extent, though, it was also testimony to his upper-class distaste for the vulgar posturing of those Indian politicians, like the Extremist Bipin Pal, whom he did hear speak at Cambridge. Whatever the reasons, Jawaharlal Nehru, far from being a prominent Indian student figure, "showed at this time," in the words of his sympathetic biographer Gopal, "no real signs of any sort of fire or distinction, and did not stand out among his generation."

He was, however, untypically for Indians of his class, an active sportsman, playing tennis, riding proficiently, and coxing a boat at races on the Cam. There is no record of his being the man-about-town he liked to pretend he was, though he is said once to have danced with a waitress just to find out what she would talk to him about. While still at Cambridge Jawaharlal joined the Inner Temple to prepare for admission to the bar, more in fulfillment of Motilal's aspirations for him than out of any great passion for the law. This entailed a move to London and studies at the London School of Economics, where it is assumed he imbibed something of the socialism that came to define his view of the world. Again, there is less evidence of an intellectual engagement with Fabianism than of his spending much of his time on more leisurely pursuits, in particular attending a number of classical music concerts. "My general attitude to life at the time," he later wrote, "was a vague kind of Cyrenaicism. . . . It is easy and gratifying to give a long Greek name to the desire for a soft life and pleasant experiences." Jawaharlal ran up a few debts along the way, once pawning his gold watch and chain, and had to seek supplementary funds from Motilal. (He could be quite manipulative in his demands, at one stage threatening to return home without finishing his studies if funds were not wired to him.) His lack of enthusiasm for his father's profession was manifest in his barely passing the bar examinations, but pass them he did, qualifying to practice law in 1912.

About to return home for good at twenty-two, Jawaharlal Nehru had completed an unremarkable first phase of his life, the only period which would not be marked by any accomplishment worthy of the name. And yet it is striking how the correspondence between father and son reveals Motilal's faith in his son's destiny. Motilal, a man of monumental self-assurance and incandescent temper, known for erupting in rage and thrashing his servants, comes across as gentle, loving, almost sentimental in his tenderness for his son — and throughout the correspondence he makes no secret of his ambitions for, and expectations of, Jawaharlal. An early postcard bearing the pictures of Congress leaders bears, just below the portrait of Romesh Chunder Dutt, Congress president in 1899 and an extraordinary figure of the age (one of the first Indians to qualify for the British-run civil service, Dutt had been a successful administrator, lawyer, historian, litterateur, and translator), the notation by Motilal: "Future Jawaharlal Nehru." If the father set the ultimate bar very high, he also urged his son to seek smaller successes, from becoming Senior Wrangler at school to taking the Indian Civil Service (ICS) examinations (which Jawaharlal in fact never did). Motilal's letters were full of advice on everything from the importance of riding and shooting to the need to avoid soccer injuries. They also dispensed opinion and insight on Indian political developments, challenging Jawaharlal to contestation and argument.

Across thousands of miles, father and son maintained a dialogue fuller and more direct than that which they might have been able to sustain had they lived under the same roof in India.

Motilal also generously funded his spendthrift son, rewarding him handsomely for every educational attainment, however modest. Every time he bridled at his son's profligacy, Jawaharlal managed to win him round. (On one such occasion Motilal wrote: "You know as well as anyone else does that, whatever my shortcomings may be, and I know there are many, I cannot be guilty of either love of money or want of love for you.") It was one of Motilal's lavish gifts — a graduation present of a hundred pounds — that nearly ended Jawaharlal Nehru's career. Urged by Motilal to spend the money visiting France and learning the language, Jawaharlal chose instead to go trekking in the Norwegian mountains with an unnamed English friend. Dipping into a stream, the young Nehru, numbed by the icy water, was swept away by a current toward a steep waterfall and would have drowned but for the pluck and enterprise of his traveling companion, who ran along the riverbank and caught him just in time, grasping a flailing leg and pulling him out of the water a few yards ahead of a four-hundred-foot drop.

This episode led a recent biographer, the American historian Stanley Wolpert, to suggest that Jawaharlal Nehru had had a homosexual relationship with his savior. Wolpert's conclusions are based, however, on so elaborate a drawing out of the circumstances, and such extensive speculation (on grounds as flimsy as Jawaharlal's tutor Brooks having been a disciple of a notorious pederast), that they are difficult to take seriously. Certainly there is no corroborating evidence, either in letters or the accounts of contemporaries, to substantiate Wolpert's claim of homosexuality. It was quite common in those days for young men to travel in pairs on the Continent, and difficult to imagine that friends, family, and acquaintances would have made no reference to homosexual tendencies if Jawaharlal had indeed been inclined that way. Nor did any chroniclers of the adult Nehru, including enemies who would have used such a charge to wound him, ever allude to any rumors of adolescent homosexuality.

By the time he embarked for India in August 1912 after nearly seven years in England, Jawaharlal Nehru had little to show for the experience: he was, in his own words, "a bit of a prig with little to commend me." Had he been better at taking exams, he might well have followed his father's initial wishes and joined the Indian Civil Service, but his modest level of academic achievement made it clear he stood no chance of succeeding in the demanding ICS examinations. Had he joined the ICS, a career in the upper reaches of the civil service might have followed, rather than in the political fray. Officials did not become statesmen; it is one of the ironies of history that had Jawaharlal Nehru been a higher achiever in his youth, he might never have attained the political heights he did in adulthood.

But there had certainly been an intangible change in the young man, for all the modesty of his scholarly accomplishment. In a moving letter upon leaving his son at Harrow, Motilal had described his pain in being separated from "the dearest treasure we have in this world . . . for your own good":

> It is not a question of providing for you, as I can do that perhaps in one single year's income. It is a question of making a real man of you. . . . It would be extremely selfish . . . to keep you with us and leave you a fortune in gold with little or no education.

Seven years later, the son confirmed that he had understood and fulfilled his father's intent. "To my mind," Jawaharlal wrote to his father four months before leaving England, in April 1912, "education does not consist of passing examinations or knowing English or mathematics. It is a mental state." In his case this was the mental state of an educated Englishman of culture and means, a product of two of the finest institutions of learning in the Empire (the same two, he would later note with pride, that had produced Lord Byron), with the attitudes that such institutions instill in their alumnae. Jawaharlal Nehru may only have had a second-class degree, but in this sense he had had a first-class English education.

The foundations had been laid, however unwittingly, for the future nationalist leader. It would hardly be surprising that Jawaharlal Nehru, having imbibed a sense of the rights of Englishmen, would one day be outraged by the realization that these rights could not be his because he was not English enough to enjoy them under British rule in India.

2

"Greatness Is Being Thrust upon Me": 1912–1921

The return home of the not-quite-prodigal, not-yet-prodigious Jawaharlal Nehru, B.A. (Cantab.), LL.B., was a major occasion for the Nehru family. When he stepped off the boat in Bombay, he was greeted by a relative; the family, with a retinue of some four dozen servants, awaited him at the hill station of Mussoorie, where his ailing mother had gone to escape the heat of the plains. Jawaharlal took a train to Dehra Dun, where he alighted into the warm embrace of a visibly moved Motilal. Both father and son then rode up to the huge mansion Motilal had rented for the occasion, and there was, if accounts of the moment are to be believed, something improbably heroic about the dashing young man cantering up the drive to reclaim his destiny. The excited women and girls rushed outside to greet him. Leaping out of the saddle and flinging the reins to a groom, Jawaharlal scarcely paused for breath as he ran to hug his mother, literally sweeping her off her feet in his joy. He was home.

He was soon put to work in his father's chambers, where his first fee as a young lawyer was the then princely sum of five hundred rupees, offered by one of Motilal's regular clients, the wealthy Rao Maharajsingh. "The first fee your father got," Motilal noted wryly, "was Rs. 5 (five only). You are evidently a hundred times better than your father." The older man must have understood perfectly well that his client's gesture was aimed at Motilal himself; his pride in his son was well enough known that people assumed that kindness to the as yet untested son was a sure way to the father's heart. As he had done at Harrow, Jawaharlal worked hard at his briefs, but his confidence faltered when he had to argue his cases in court, and he was not considered much of a success. It did not help that his interest in the law was at best tepid and that he found much of the work assigned to him "pointless and futile," his cases "petty and rather dull."

Jawaharlal sought to escape the tedium of his days by partying extravagantly at night, a habit encouraged by his father's own penchant for lavish entertainment. He called on assorted members of Allahabad's high society, leaving his card at various English homes. But he made no great mark upon what even his authorized biographer called "the vacuous, parasitic life of upper-middle-class society in Allahabad." At his own home, Jawaharlal played the role of the dominant elder brother. He tormented his little sister Betty, startling her horse to teach her to hold her nerve, or throwing her into the deep end of the pool to force her to learn to swim. These lessons served more to instill fear than courage in the little girl. He took holidays in Kashmir, on one occasion going on a hunt and shooting an antelope that died at his feet, its "great big eyes full of tears" — a sight that would haunt Jawaharlal for years.

All told, however, there was little of note about Jawaharlal Nehru's first few years back in India, until his marriage — arranged, of course, by his father — in February 1916. Father and son had dealt with the subject of marriage in their transcontinental correspondence, but Motilal had given short shrift to Jawaharlal's mild demurrals whenever the matter was broached. In a letter to his mother Jawaharlal had even suggested he might prefer to remain unmarried rather than plight his troth to someone he did not like: "I accept that any girl selected by you and father would be good in all respects, but still, I may not be able to get along well with her." But for all the romantic idealism in his epistolary descriptions of the ideal marriage, he gave in to his parents' wishes. For his parents, there was no question of allowing the young man to choose his own bride; quite apart from the traditional practice of arranging marriages, Motilal took a particular interest in seeing that his son was well settled. "It is all right, my boy," he wrote to Jawaharlal as early as 1907 on the subject. "You may leave your future happiness in my hands and rest assured that to secure that is the one object of my ambition."

The Nehrus launched an extensive search within the Kashmiri Pandit community before settling on Kamala

Kaul, the daughter of a flour-mill owner. When the decision was made Jawaharlal had not yet returned to India and Kamala herself was barely thirteen. Needless to say, they had never met. She spoke not a word of English, having been educated in Hindi and Urdu, and had none of the graces required for the Westernized society Jawaharlal frequented, so Motilal arranged for her to be groomed for his son by Nan's and Betty's English governesses. Three years of "finishing" later, on the auspicious day of Vasant Panchami, which marks the first full moon of spring, and which fell that year (1916) on February 8, Jawaharlal Nehru, twenty-six, married Kamala Kaul, ten years his junior. It was, at least in one crucial respect, a match made in heaven: Jawaharlal's mother had insisted on comparing the astrological charts of the young couple, which a pundit she trusted assured her were compatible.

For Allahabad high society, the wedding was the grandest event of 1916 — but it took place in Delhi. Motilal rented an entire train to transport family and friends to the new capital city of India (a status Delhi had acquired, at Calcutta's expense, in 1911), where a "Nehru marriage camp" was set up in style. The celebrations lasted a week in Delhi and were repeated in an endless round of parties, concerts, and poetry recitals in honor of the young couple when they came back to Allahabad.

Jawaharlal left Kamala behind when he went trekking and hunting with friends in Kashmir that summer and had his second narrow escape from an untimely death. Exhausted by almost twelve hours of continuous mountain climbing, and seeking to cross an ice field,

Jawaharlal stepped on a pile of fresh snow: "it gave way and down I went into a huge and yawning crevasse. . . . But the rope held and I clutched to [*sic*] the side of the crevasse and was pulled out."

Jawaharlal Nehru had not been saved for a life of mediocre lawyering and relentless socializing. Three years after his return to India, he was bored by both pursuits. Politics began to command more and more of his attention. For several years, the Indian National Congress had been run by the Moderates, who contented themselves with the ritual adoption of resolutions exhorting their British rulers to do better by India. While this kind of politics did not enthuse Jawaharlal, neither was he greatly inspired by the Extremists, who had split from the party and established Home Rule Leagues around the country seeking self-government for India within the Empire. But the Extremist leader Annie Besant had been an old family friend, having helped initiate him as a thirteen-year-old into theosophy. So Jawaharlal joined her Home Rule League and made his first public speech on June 20, 1916 in Mrs. Besant's defense and in protest of the Press Act,[1] under which she had been prosecuted.

[1] The Press Act of 1910 was a key instrument of British control of Indian public opinion. Under its provisions an established press or newspaper had to provide a security deposit of up to five thousand rupees (a considerable sum in those days); a new publication would have to pay up to two thousand. If the newspaper printed something of which the government disapproved, the money could be forfeit, the press closed down, and its proprietors and editors prosecuted. Annie Besant had refused to pay a security on a paper she published advocating home rule, and was arrested for failing to do so and thereby violating the Act.

It was a modest performance, with no immediate consequences. Father and son attended the Lucknow Congress of 1916, where a historic Hindu-Muslim pact was concluded between the Indian National Congress and the Muslim League, a party of Muslim notables that had been established in 1905 to advance Muslim interests (though several leading Congressmen, including three of the party's presidents to date, were themselves Muslim). But Jawaharlal did not speak at the Congress, remaining on the margins of that great (and sadly to prove evanescent) triumph of Hindu-Muslim political cooperation.

His father, however, was emerging as a major figure in the party. Motilal was named by the Congress to draft, together with a brilliant young Muslim lawyer called Mohammed Ali Jinnah, the principles that would govern cooperation with the Muslim League. Their work, recognizing the principle that decisions would not be taken affecting the interests and beliefs of a minority community without the agreement of a majority of that community's representatives, formed the foundation of what was widely hailed as the Lucknow Pact. The Congress's leading literary light, the poetess Sarojini Naidu, hailed Jinnah as the "ambassador of Hindu-Muslim unity" and set about editing a compilation of his speeches and writings. Nineteen-sixteen was a banner year for the nationalist movement. The fracture in the Congress between the Moderates and the Extremists had been overcome with the reentry of Tilak and Besant into the party; now the chasm between the Congress and the Muslim League appeared to have been bridged as well. Jinnah declared that, after the Great War was over, "India will have to be granted her birthright as a free, responsible and equal member of the British Empire."

Had the British found the wisdom to embrace this demand, Jinnah might well have emerged as prime minister of an Indian Dominion within the Empire around 1918; the full independence of India from the British Raj might have been greatly delayed; Hindu-Muslim clashes leading to the partition of the country might not have occurred; and the political career of Jawaharlal Nehru might have taken a very different course. But imperial Britain had no intention of accommodating the aspirations of its Indian subjects, and it reacted to the moderate nationalism of what Jinnah called "the united India demand" by the half-hearted Montagu-Chemsford reforms,[2] which even the Moderates found unacceptable, and by the more familiar method of repression.

When the outspoken Mrs. Besant was interned by the British authorities in 1917 for seditious activity, Jawaharlal abandoned any remaining hesitancy about his opposition to the British Raj in India. Though an office-bearer of the provincial Home Rule League, he had

[2]The Montagu-Chelmsford reforms, named for the secretary of state for India and the viceroy, constituted the Government of India Act passed after the First World War to "reward" India for its support of the British in that conflict. Whereas Indians had expected Dominion status analogous to the arrangements prevailing in Australia, Canada, New Zealand, and South Africa — or at the very least significant progress toward self-government — they received instead a system of "dyarchy" which associated Indians with some institutions of government but left power solidly in the viceroy's hands.

considered playing a leading part in a meeting to expand an Indian Defense Force, based on the British notion of a Territorial Army, and had even applied to enlist in such a reserve; but with Annie Besant's arrest he withdrew his application, and the meeting itself was cancelled. Instead Jawaharlal published a letter in a leading newspaper calling for noncooperation with the government. But he did not initially have a clear idea of what that would involve; in 1918 he moved a resolution at the United Provinces Political Conference criticizing the British government for its refusal to permit an Indian delegation to travel to London to argue the case for home rule. Only later did the realization dawn on him that home rule would not come about by pleading with the British. In early 1919 he signed a pledge not to obey the Anarchical and Revolutionary Crimes Act (the "Rowlatt Act"),[3] and joined a committee to propagate that pledge — the satyagraha vow, as it was known. Satyagraha, or "truth force," was a new concept in Indian nationalist politics, introduced by a thin, bespectacled lawyer wearing coarse homespun, Mohandas Karamchand Gandhi, who in 1915 had returned to India from a long sojourn in South Africa, where his "experiments with truth" and his morally charged leadership of the

[3]The Rowlatt Act, perhaps the most oppressive piece of legislation passed by the British government in India, established summary procedures for dealing with political agitation, including punishments by whipping, imprisonment, fines, forfeiture of property, and death. It also sharply limited the rights of defendants in sedition trials, thus antagonizing British-trained lawyers as well as fervent Indian nationalists.

Indian diaspora had earned him the sobriquet of Mahatma ("Great Soul").

Starting off as a not particularly gifted lawyer engaged by an Indian in South Africa to plead a routine case, Gandhi had developed into a formidable figure. Appalled by the racial discrimination to which his countrymen were subject in South Africa, Gandhi had embarked upon a series of legal and political actions designed to protest and overturn the iniquities the British and the Boers imposed upon Indians. After his attempts to petition the authorities for justice (and to curry their favor by organizing a volunteer ambulance brigade of Indians) had proved ineffective, Gandhi developed a unique method of resistance through civil disobedience. His talent for organization (he founded the Indian National Congress in Natal) was matched by an equally rigorous penchant for self-examination and philosophical inquiry. Instead of embracing the bourgeois comforts that his status in the Indian community of South Africa might have entitled him to, Gandhi retreated to a communal farm he established outside Durban, read Thoreau, and corresponded with the likes of Ruskin and Tolstoy, all the while seeking to arrive at an understanding of "truth" in both personal life and public affairs. The journey from petition politics to satyagraha was neither short nor easy, but having made it and then returned to his native land, the Mahatma brought to the incipient nationalist movement of India an extraordinary reputation as both saint and strategist.

Gandhi's singular insight was that self-government would never be achieved by the resolutions passed by a self-regarding and unelected elite pursuing the politics of the drawingroom. To him, self-government had to involve the empowerment of the masses, the toiling multitudes of India in whose name the upper classes were clamoring for home rule. This position did not go over well with India's political class, which consisted in those days largely of maharajahs and lawyers, men of means who discoursed in English and demanded the rights of Englishmen. Nor did Gandhi's insistence that the masses be mobilized not by the methods of "princes and potentates" (his phrase) but by moral values derived from ancient tradition and embodied in swadeshi (self-reliance on indigenous products) and satyagraha.

To put his principles into practice, the Mahatma lived a simple life of near-absolute poverty in an ashram and traveled across the land in third-class railway compartments, campaigning against untouchability, poor sanitation, and child marriage, and preaching an eclectic set of virtues from sexual abstinence to the weaving of *khadi* (a coarse homespun cloth) and the beneficial effects of frequent enemas. That he was an eccentric seemed beyond doubt; that he had touched a chord among the masses was equally apparent; that he was a potent political force soon became clear. His crusade against the system of indentured labor that had transported Indians to British colonies across the world so moved the public, poor and rich alike, that the viceroy of India put an end to it in 1917 (it was formally abolished in 1920).

Gandhi next turned his attention to the appalling conditions of indigo farmers in the north Indian district of Champaran, where he agitated for better terms for the peasant cultivators who had long been oppressed by English planters and British laws. More important, he captured the imagination of the nation by publicly breaking English law in the name of a higher law ("the voice of conscience") and challenging the British to imprison him. The British, not desirous of making a martyr of the Mahatma, dropped all charges — and made him a national hero instead.

It was when the British passed the Rowlatt Act in March 1919 suspending the rights of defendants in sedition trials that Gandhi, despite being seriously ill with dysentery, conceived of the satyagraha pledge that Jawaharlal Nehru signed in April. The younger man was rapidly converted to the Mahatma's zeal and commitment to action. Motilal, though equally contemptuous of legislation that most educated Indians called the "Black Act," and willing to challenge the law in the courts, was dismayed by his son's willingness to disobey it in the streets. They argued furiously about Motilal's conviction that Jawaharlal should not break the law because doing so would make him a criminal. But Jawaharlal was not swayed. His apparent determination to follow Gandhi's call first appalled, then moved, his father: Motilal, who thought the very idea of going to jail was "preposterous," decided to join his son if he could not dissuade him, and secretly slept on the floor to prepare himself for the rigors of the imprisonment he knew would follow. But as ever, Motilal did not give up easily. As a wise father, he had one last trump up his sleeve. He invited Mahatma Gandhi to visit him in Allahabad in March 1919. After long conversations between the two older men at Anand Bhavan, Gandhi advised Jawaharlal to put his love for and duty toward his father ahead of his commitment to satyagraha. The shrewd Mahatma had perhaps realized that the Indian nationalist movement would need both Nehrus, and sought to avoid alienating the father by winning over his son too soon.

So the younger Nehru did not get to follow the Mahatma to jail, or even to his ashram. Jawaharlal was increasingly spending time on journalistic pursuits, first for the *Leader*, a newspaper controlled by his father, and then for the *Independent*, founded by Motilal when the *Leader*'s editor won a boardroom battle over his opposition to the increasingly confrontationist line Motilal wished him to follow. Jawaharlal even edited the *Independent* for a while, before surrendering the reins to the fiery (and, as it turned out, irresponsible) Bipin Chandra Pal. Though the paper lost a great deal of Motilal's money and would eventually have to be closed, it gave Jawaharlal an opportunity to hone his skills as an essayist and polemicist. At last the English education was put to good use; the experience shaped a gift for words which would leave the world with some of the finest political writing to emerge from India in the twentieth century.

The event that sealed the fate of the British Raj in India, that underlined Gandhi's leadership of the national movement, and that irrevocably brought Jawaharlal and Motilal Nehru to the conviction that nothing short of independence was acceptable, occurred on April 13, 1919, in the town of Amritsar in the province of Punjab. It was Baisakhi, the major spring holiday, and more than ten thousand people had gathered in a walled open area, the Jallianwalla Bagh, for a peaceful gathering of satyagrahis protesting British iniquities. Brigadier General R. E. H. Dyer, the newly arrived local military commander, saw the meeting as an affront and the crowd of unarmed men and women, some with their families, as an incipient mob. He ordered his troops to take up positions around the enclosure, from which there was only a single narrow exit. And though there is no record of any act by the crowd, any provocation that could be cited as triggering his decision, Dyer ordered his men, standing behind the brick walls surrounding the Bagh, to level their rifles at the assembled men, women, and children barely 150 yards away and fire.

There was no warning, no announcement that the gathering was illegal and had to disperse, no instruction to leave peacefully: nothing. Dyer did not order his men to fire in the air, or at the feet of their targets. They fired, at his orders, into the chests, the faces, and the wombs of the unarmed and defenseless crowd.

History knows the event as the Amritsar Massacre. The label connotes the heat and fire of slaughter, the butchery by bloodthirsty fighters of an outgunned opposition. But there was nothing of this at Jallianwalla Bagh. Dyer's soldiers were lined up calmly, almost routinely; they were neither threatened nor attacked by the crowd; it was just another day's work, but one unlike any other. They loaded and fired their rifles coldly, clinically, without haste or passion or sweat or anger, emptying their magazines into the shrieking, wailing, then stampeding crowd with trained precision. As people sought to flee the horror toward the single exit, they were trapped in a murderous fusillade. Sixteen hundred bullets were fired that day into the unarmed throng, and when the job was finished, just ten minutes later, 379 people lay dead and 1,137 lay injured, many grotesquely maimed for life. A total of 1,516 casualties from 1,600 bullets: only 84 had failed to find their mark, a measure of how simple, and how brutal, Dyer's task was.

The Amritsar Massacre was no act of insane frenzy but a conscious, deliberate imposition of colonial will. Dyer was an efficient killer rather than a crazed maniac; his was merely the evil of the unimaginative, the brutality of the military bureaucrat. But his action that Baisakhi day came to symbolize the evil of the system on whose behalf, and in whose defense, he was acting. In the horrified realization of this truth by Indians of all walks of life lay the true importance of the Amritsar Massacre. It represented the worst that colonialism could become, and by letting it occur, the British crossed that point of no return that exists only in the minds of men — that point which, in any unequal relationship, both master and subject must instinctively respect if their relationship is to survive.

The massacre made Indians out of millions of people who had not thought consciously of their political identity before that grim Sunday. It turned loyalists into nationalists and constitutionalists into agitators, led the Nobel Prize–winning poet Rabindranath Tagore to return his knighthood to the king and a host of Indian appointees to British offices to turn in their commissions. And above all it entrenched in Mahatma Gandhi a firm and unshakable faith in the moral righteousness of the cause of Indian independence. He now saw freedom as indivisible from Truth (itself a concept he imbued with greater meaning than can be found in any dictionary), and he never wavered in his commitment to ridding India of an empire he saw as irremediably evil, even satanic.

While the official commission of inquiry largely whitewashed Dyer's conduct, Motilal Nehru was appointed by the Congress to head a public inquiry into the atrocity, and he sent his son to Amritsar to look into the facts. Jawaharlal's diary meticulously records his findings; at one point he counted sixty-seven bullet marks on one part of a wall. He visited the lane where Indians had been ordered by the British to crawl on their bellies and pointed out in the press that the crawling had not even been on hands and knees but fully on the ground, in "the manner of snakes and worms." On his return journey to Delhi by train he found himself sharing a compartment with Dyer and a group of British military officers. Dyer boasted, in Nehru's own account, that "he had [had] the whole town at his mercy and he had felt like reducing the rebellious city to a heap of ashes, but he took pity on it and refrained. . . . I was greatly shocked to hear his conversation and to observe his callous manner."

The son's investigations drew him even closer politically to his father. Motilal was elected president of the Congress session of 1919, which took place, deliberately, in Amritsar. The massacre dispelled some of his doubts about Gandhi's doctrine of noncooperation; henceforward he joined his son in accepting that the British had left little room for an alternative. For Jawaharlal, the English reaction to the massacre — Dyer was publicly feted, and a collection raised for him among English expatriates in India brought him the quite stupendous sum of a quarter of a million pounds — was almost as bad as the massacre itself. "This cold-blooded approval of that deed shocked me greatly," he later wrote. "It seemed absolutely immoral, indecent; to use public school language, it was the height of bad form. I realized then, more vividly than I had ever done before, how brutal and immoral imperialism was and how it had eaten into the souls of the British upper classes."

In early 1920 Mahatma Gandhi embarked on the Khilafat movement, which rallied Hindus and Muslims together on the somewhat obscure platform of demanding the restoration of the Caliphate in Turkey. Gandhi did not particularly want a religious figurehead to take over the dissolving Ottoman Empire in preference to a secularizing figure (such as later emerged in the person of Kemal Ataturk), but he saw that the issue mattered to several Indian Muslim leaders and he wished to seize the opportunity to consolidate the Hindu-Muslim unity that had emerged over the previous four years. Jawaharlal's secular instincts would ordinarily have put him on the opposite side of this issue, but he saw the political merits of the movement and wrote articles in the *Independent* depicting the Khilafat movement as an integral part of the ongoing political struggle for Asia's freedom. The agitation briefly inspired the masses, many of whom had no real idea where Turkey was or why the Khilafat mattered. It also brought anti-British Muslims into the Congress, since many Muslim Leaguers were allied with the government and unwilling to oppose it for the sake of the caliph. But as a modernizing Turkey itself turned away from the cause, it petered out as a significant issue in Indian politics.

Meanwhile, the death of Tilak and the official launching of Gandhi's noncooperation movement, both on August 1, 1920, marked the Mahatma's ascension to unchallenged leadership of the Indian National Congress. (Gokhale had died earlier, in 1915, at the shockingly young age of forty-nine.) The special session of the Congress in Calcutta that year saw the entire old guard of the party arrayed against Gandhi, but as the debates progressed and the Mahatma clung stubbornly to the dictates of his conscience, the leadership realized they needed him more than he needed them. Gandhi's program passed in committee with strong Muslim support and the surprising defection from the old guard of Motilal Nehru; it was then resoundingly adopted by the plenary. This was a defeat, above all, for Jinnah, the principal epitome of the old "drawingroom" politics, who wrote to the Mahatma to deplore his appeal to "the inexperienced youth and the ignorant and the illiterate. All this means complete disorganization and chaos. What the consequences of this may be, I shudder to contemplate." His disillusionment with Gandhi's mass mobilization led to Jinnah's gradual withdrawal from political life — booed off the stage at the 1920 Nagpur Congress, he took the next train to Delhi, never to return to the party — and later, in 1930, to bitter, if comfortable, self-exile in England. When he returned, it would be to challenge everything that Gandhi stood for.

But Jawaharlal was thrilled by the Mahatma's triumph.

Some have suggested that Motilal's shift to the pro-Gandhi side at Calcutta was prompted by his regard for his son, whose affections he feared he would otherwise have lost. The Khilafat movement and noncooperation prompted Jawaharlal also to follow Gandhi's call to boycott the legislative councils for which elections were to be held under the Montagu-Chelmsford reforms. Motilal had been leading the Congress's election effort in the province and only reluctantly acquiesced in the party's decision — which his son had strongly urged — to boycott the elections. Jawaharlal was soon a leading figure in the United Provinces (U.P.)[4] noncooperation movement, organizing drills for volunteers and casting aside his diffidence to address large crowds. His message was simple: "there was no middle course left; one was with either the country or its enemies, either with Gandhi or the Government." His first direct clash with the government occurred in May 1920 when he was on holiday with his family in Mussoorie and was asked by the police to provide an undertaking not to contact an Afghan delegation which was staying at the same hotel. Though Jawaharlal had had no intention of meeting the Afghans — whom the British suspected of being in India to lend support to the Khilafat movement — he refused to furnish such an undertaking, and was duly externed from Mussoorie. Jawaharlal accepted his expulsion; for all his admiration for the Mahatma, he was not yet

[4]The acronym "U.P." so entered the Indian consciousness that after independence the government renamed the state Uttar Pradesh (Northern Province) in order to retain the initials.

politician enough, or Gandhian enough, to defy the police and court arrest — much to the relief of Motilal, who feared the consequences to the family of such an action.

These were difficult times for Motilal. He had given up his legal practice at the peak of his career to devote himself to politics, but it saddened him to see his son, in his prime, embracing Gandhian austerity and traveling in third-class railway carriages. The loss of a steady income from what had been a flourishing practice meant that the comforts of life were being denied his family. (Some of this was by choice: the closing of the wine cellar, the exchange of the Savile Row suits for homespun khadi, the replacement of three English meals a day by one simple Indian lunch.)

Jawaharlal's daughter, Indira Priyadarshini, was born on November 19, 1917, but was receiving little attention from her increasingly politically active father. (Her admirably simple first name, though, was something Jawaharlal may well have insisted upon. He had never liked his own polysyllabic and traditional appellation, once writing to a friend: "for heaven's sake don't call your son Jawaharlal. Jawahar [*jewel*] by itself might pass, but the addition of 'lal' [*precious*] makes it odious.") Childbirth at eighteen left Kamala weak and ill, and her husband's neglect could not have improved matters for her. On one occasion Jawaharlal failed to decipher a prescription the Nehru family homeopath had written for his wife, and Motilal snapped: "There is nothing very complicated about Dr. Ray's letter if you will only read it carefully after divesting your mind of Khilafat and Satyagraha."

Jawaharlal was, typically, blissfully unconscious of the financial burdens his own father had to bear, cheerfully donating to the Congress cause the war bonds Motilal had put aside for his inheritance. Motilal finally closed the *Independent* in 1921, unable to sustain its continuing losses. Too proud to draw a salary for his political work, Motilal decided to resume his legal practice so that his family would be provided for. Jawaharlal, enthralled by Gandhian self-denial, cared little about such matters, provoking his father to declare bluntly: "You cannot have it both ways: Insist on my having no money and yet expect me to pay you money."

But Jawaharlal was not merely feckless. He immersed himself with compassion in the cause of the landless peasantry of U.P., taking on the vice presidency of the Kisan Sabha (Farmers' Council) and lending his advocacy and his pen to their grievances. He began, too, to show some of the emotional identification with them that would forever characterize his relationship with the Indian masses. "I have had the privilege of working for them," he wrote in 1921, "of mixing with them, of living in their mud huts and partaking in all reverence of their lowly fare. . . . I have come to believe that Nonviolence is ingrained in them and is part of their very nature." Such feelings marked the beginning of the Harrovian and Cantabrigian Nehru's rediscovery of India, and of his own Indianness — a process (as the reference to Nonviolence underlined) that was intertwined with his admiration of Mahatma Gandhi. He "found the whole countryside afire with enthusiasm and full of a strange excitement. Enormous gatherings would take place at the briefest notice by word of mouth." Roads would be built for him overnight to allow his car to pass; when his wheels got stuck in the soft mud, villagers would bodily lift his vehicle onto drier ground. "Looking at them and their misery and overflowing gratitude, I was filled with shame and sorrow, shame at my own easygoing and comfortable life and our petty politics of the city which ignored this vast multitude of semi-naked sons and daughters of India, sorrow at the degradation and overwhelming poverty of India."

Though the emotional intensity was genuine, the political opportunity was there to be seized. Jawaharlal sought to harness the peasants to the Congress's nationalist cause and helped organize Kisan Sabhas, or farmers' associations (though the U.P. Kisan Sabha itself split in early 1921 over the issue of noncooperation). His old shyness was now completely overcome; in its place arose the mounting oratorical confidence of an increasingly surefooted politician. After one episode where a number of farmers were killed by unprovoked police firing, Jawaharlal calmed matters by persuading angry farmers to disperse rather than to resort to violence in their turn. The episode pointed both to his increasing capacity for leadership and discipline as well as his instinct for moderation; Jawaharlal the Congress organizer was not quite the firebrand that Jawaharlal the Congress polemicist had suggested he might be.

The peasantry of U.P., whose backbreaking work under wretched conditions was exploited both by Indian landlords (zamindars) and the British administration, were in many ways ripe for revolt, but Jawaharlal was no

Bolshevik (the one threat some of the British expected and feared). He preached unity between kisans and zamindars, rejected calls by peasant agitators for nonpayment of rents, and constantly extolled Mahatma Gandhi's message of nonviolence and self-reliance. He romanticized the Indian farmer as a sort of local equivalent of the sturdy and honest English yeoman; but he saw India's peasant masses as a base of support for nationalist politics, not as fodder for agrarian revolution. Time after time he urged angry crowds to calm down, to call off protests, to acquiesce in an arrest rather than to resist it. Like Gandhi, he was mobilizing the masses for responsible ends.

"Greatness," Jawaharlal wrote to his father at the time of the Mussoorie Afghan episode, "is being thrust upon me." The words may have been slightly ironic at the time, but they were to prove prophetic.

3

"To Suffer for the Dear Country": 1921–1928

In 1920, Gandhi declared that India would have *swaraj* (self-government) within a year, a promise Jawaharlal Nehru described as "delightfully vague." Less vague was the slogan that drove Gandhi's followers in the civil disobedience movement of 1921: "Go to the villages!" Jawaharlal found himself traveling to impassioned meetings in rural areas (by car, train, and horse-drawn carriage, and once on an improvised trolley sent wheeling down the railway track after he had missed his train), calling for freedom for India, the restoration of the Khilafat in Turkey, and economic self-reliance (to be achieved through boycotting foreign goods, spinning khadi at home and consigning English suits to the bonfire). Nonviolence, Hindu-Muslim unity, harmony between tenants and landlords, and the abolition of untouchability were the pillars of the movement on which Gandhi had launched the nation. "Noncooperation" with the British was the slogan, but like so many other Indian political negatives, from nonviolence to nonalignment, it was imbued with a positive content transcending that which it sought to negate.

Jawaharlal Nehru, no longer the diffident political neophyte, plunged himself into the campaign with great zeal. He revealed, or at any rate developed, a talent for both oratory and organization: when on one occasion a government order was served on him prohibiting him from addressing a meeting, he marched four and a half miles with the entire assemblage to the next district and resumed his speech there. He formed and drilled volunteer squads, inspiring them to paralyze life in various U.P. towns through "hartals," or work stoppages, in the name of noncooperation with the colonial authorities. The mounting momentum behind these efforts caused alarm among British officialdom, already tense about the impending visit to India of the Prince of Wales. On December 6, 1921, both Motilal and Jawaharlal Nehru were arrested, each for the first time in his life.

Jawaharlal had spent part of the morning at the district court attending the trial of fellow Congressman K. D. Malaviya. "The poor judge [was] in a bad way," he wrote in his diary. "He appeared to be the convict and the prisoners the judges." When father and son were taken away by the police, Motilal issued a message to his compatriots: "Having served you to the best of my ability, it is now my high privilege to serve the motherland by going to jail with my only son." Jawaharlal was taken to Lucknow for detention and trial, principally for his leadership of the volunteers, whose organization had been declared illegal. He was sentenced (under the wrong section of the penal code, as it later turned out) to six months in prison and a fine of a hundred rupees or a further month of imprisonment. Motilal, after a farcical trial in which an illiterate witness "verified" his signature on a seditious document while holding it upside down, was sentenced to six months' imprisonment and a five-hundred-rupee fine. (His refusal to pay the fine resulted in the seizure of property from his home worth several times that amount.) Both father and son, in their separate jail cells, declined the special privileges offered to them in view of their social standing. Jawaharlal relished his status as a prisoner of the Raj. A fellow Congress worker noted that "the smiling and happy countenance of Pandit Jawaharlal Nehru stood out in relief amongst the persons in the lock-up."

It was not to last. The increasing violence of the noncooperation movement, and in particular the murder of two dozen policemen by a nationalist mob in the small U.P. town of Chauri Chaura on February 5, 1922, led Mahatma Gandhi to call off the agitation, fearing that his followers were not yet ready for the nonviolent attainment of freedom. Thanks to a technical error in his sentencing, Jawaharlal was released in March 1922, with only half his sentence served. He was bitterly disappointed with Gandhi's decision and its effect on his volunteers, who had made such headway in destabilizing British rule in U.P. But his faith in the Mahatma remained, and he wrote to his colleague Syed Mahmud:

"You will be glad to learn that work is flourishing. We are laying sure foundations this time. . . . [T]here will be no relaxation, no lessening in our activities and above all there will be no false compromise with Government. We stand," he added in a Gandhian touch, "for the truth."

It is said that Motilal enjoyed such close relations with the British governor of U.P., Sir Harcourt Butler, that during his first imprisonment he received a daily half-bottle of champagne brought personally to the prison by the governor's aide-de-camp. With his father still in jail, Jawaharlal continued his efforts to promote disaffection with British rule, and for his pains he was arrested again on May 12, 1922. Refusing to defend himself, he issued an emotional and colorful statement: "India will be free; of that there is no doubt. . . . Jail has indeed become a heaven for us, a holy place of pilgrimage since our saintly and beloved leader was sentenced. . . . I marvel at my good fortune. To serve India in the battle of freedom is honor enough. To serve her under a leader like Mahatma Gandhi is doubly fortunate. But to suffer for the dear country! What greater good fortune could befall an Indian, unless it be death for the cause or the full realization of our glorious dream?"

The British may have dismissed such words as romanticized bombast, but they struck a chord among the public beyond the courtroom, giving the thirty-three-year-old Jawaharlal Nehru national celebrity as the hero of Indian youth. The trial court was his platform, but his real audience was young Indians everywhere. By the summer of 1922, Motilal, now released and traveling across the country, found his son's fame widespread, and his already considerable pride in Jawaharlal grew even further. "On reading your statement," he wrote to his son, "I felt I was the proudest father in the world." This time the younger Nehru drew a sentence of eighteen months' rigorous imprisonment, a fine of a hundred rupees, and a further three months in jail if he did not pay the fine. There were no judicial irregularities to mitigate his punishment.

Despite poor health, which required homeopathic medication in jail, and food that was "quite amazingly bad," Jawaharlal welcomed his imprisonment. He seemed to see it as confirmation of his sacrifices for the nation, while writing to his father that no sympathy was needed for "we who laze and eat and sleep" while others "work and labor outside." He used his time to read widely — the Koran, the Bible, and the Bhagavad Gita, a history of the Holy Roman Empire, Havell's *Aryan Rule in India* with its paeans to India's glorious past, and the memoirs of the Mughal emperor Babar and the French traveler Bernier. These works fed a romanticized sense of the Indian nationalist struggle as a version of the Italian Risorgimento; in one letter he even quoted Meredith's poem on the heroes of the latter, substituting the word "India" for "Italia." This, as Gopal has observed, "was adolescent exaltation, yet to be channeled by hard thinking." Jawaharlal was suffused with "the glow of virginal suffering, . . . in love with sacrifice and hardship. . . . He had made a cradle of emotional nationalism and rocked himself in it." A British interviewer in late 1923 noted that Nehru had no "clear idea of how he proposed to win Swaraj or what he proposed to do with it when he had won it."

Once again Jawaharlal was released before he had served his full sentence, emerging from prison at the end of January 1923 following a provincial amnesty. But the premature release would be more than made up for in seven more terms of imprisonment over the next two decades, which gave him a grand total of 3,262 days in eight different jails. Nearly ten years of his life were to be wasted behind bars — though perhaps not entirely wasted, since they allowed him to produce several remarkable books of reflection, nationalist awakening, and autobiography. His first letter to his five-year-old daughter Indira (asking her whether she had "plied" her new spinning wheel yet) was written from Lucknow jail. This largely one-sided correspondence would later culminate in two monumental books painting a vivid portrait of Jawaharlal Nehru's mind and of his vision of the world.

In the meantime, the early 1920s found Indian nationalism in the doldrums. Gandhi's decision to call off the noncooperation movement was baffling to many Muslim leaders, who saw in his placing the principle of nonviolence above the exigencies of opposition to British rule a form of Hindu religious fervor that sat ill with them. This, and the fizzling out of the Khilafat movement, ended what had been the apogee of Hindu-Muslim unity in Indian politics, a period when the Muslim leader Maulana Muhammad Ali[5] could tell the Amritsar Congress in 1919: "After the Prophet, on whom be peace, I consider it my duty to carry out the demands of Gandhiji." The president of the Muslim League

[5]Not to be confused with Mohammed Ali Jinnah, Maulana Muhammad Ali (1878–1931) was a leader of the Khilafat agitation and president of the Congress in 1923.

in 1920, Dr. M. A. Ansari, had abandoned the League for the Congress; the Congress's own president in 1921, Hakim Ajmal Khan, had been a member of the original delegation of Muslim notables to the viceroy in 1906 which had first established the League. Yet by 1923 a growing estrangement between the two communities became apparent, with several Hindu-Muslim riots breaking out, notably the "Kohat killings" and the "Moplah rebellion" in opposite extremities of the country. In the twenty-two years after 1900 there had been only sixteen communal riots throughout India; in the three years thereafter, there were seventy-two. The Mahatma responded by undertaking fasts to shame his countrymen into better behavior.

During this time Jawaharlal found his leader unwilling to lead. Gandhi "refused to look into the future, or lay down any long-distance program. We were to carry on patiently 'serving' the people." This, despite the ironic quotation marks around the word "serving," Jawaharlal continued to do, focusing particularly on the boycott of foreign cloth and the promotion of homespun, a cause which bolstered Indian self-reliance while uniting peasants, weavers, and political workers under a common Congress banner. But he was too dispirited to do more than extol khadi; in particular, he took no specific steps to combat the growing communalization of politics. Devoid of religious passions himself, with many close Muslim friends whom he saw as friends first and Muslims after (if at all), he could not at this time take religious divisions seriously; he saw them as a waste of time, a distraction from the real issues at hand. "Senseless and criminal bigotry," he wrote in a speech delivered for him when he was ill in October 1923, "struts about in the name of religion and instills hatred and violence into the people." Three years later he wrote to a Muslim friend that "what is required in India most is a course of study of Bertrand Russell's books." The atheist rationalism of the British philosopher was to remain a profound influence; religion, Nehru wrote, was a "terrible burden" that India had to get rid of if it was to "breathe freely or do anything useful."

The young idealist was also disillusioned by the cliquism and intrigues which were taking over the Congress itself. Some nationalists were accepting office under the Raj; Jawaharlal himself was sounded out about becoming the provincial education minister, a suggestion to which he gave short shrift. Instead he became general secretary of the All-India Congress Committee, in which capacity he made an abortive attempt to persuade partymen to dispense with the profusion of honorifics encumbering Indian names, starting with the "Mahatma" before "Gandhi." (He was quickly slapped down by Muhammad Ali and, chastened, never repeated the attempt.)

But the party was split on a more important issue. A section of Congressmen, including Motilal Nehru and Bengal's Chitta Ranjan Das, decided to contest elections to the legislative council, which offered limited self-government to Indians in a system of "dyarchy" under British rule. They called themselves the Swaraj Party; by cooperating with the British political machinery it seemed they had resurrected the old Moderate faction from under Gandhi's suffocating embrace, though in fact they saw their role as a new form of noncooperation (since election would offer Indians the power to make legislative demands and obstruct British governance if these demands were not met). Gandhi and the majority of the Congress, however, opposed this approach, Jawaharlal among them. Motilal did not try to wean his son away from the Mahatma, but Das did, unsuccessfully. The elections of November 1923 saw the Swarajists winning convincingly, bringing the voice of Indian nationalism into the ruling councils of the Raj. But Gandhi did not approve of their participation in the colonial system, and Jawaharlal's support for him exasperated his father. In September 1924 Gandhi wrote to Motilal to say that Jawaharlal "is one of the loneliest young men of my acquaintance in India. The idea of your mental desertion of him hurts me. . . . I don't want to be the cause, direct or indirect, of the slightest breach in [your] wonderful affection."

A third round of imprisonment had meanwhile punctuated the burgeoning Nehru curriculum vitae. A nonviolent agitation by the Sikh Akali movement in the Punjab, principally aimed at wresting control of Sikh shrines from British-appointed Hindu overseers, caught Jawaharlal's attention, especially since the Sikhs' discipline in peacefully courting arrest was the effective application of a Congress tactic. In September 1923, visiting the "princely state" of Nabha (a principality nominally ruled by an Indian rajah but in fact under the control of a British Resident, or administrator) to observe the Akalis in action, Jawaharlal found himself arrested on dubious legal grounds and incarcerated in a vile cell in abominable conditions. Motilal came to visit his son and was dismayed that his courageous intervention — which included cables to the viceroy, whose office overruled the Resident and allowed him to see his son without preconditions — had only irritated Jawaharlal, who was clearly relishing the role of the unjustly imprisoned martyr. Departing unhappily, Motilal sent his son a tart letter: "I was pained to find that instead of affording you any relief, my visit of yesterday only had the effect of disturbing the even tenor of your happy jail life. After much anxious thinking I have come to the conclusion that I can do no good either to you or to myself by repeating my visits. . . . [P]lease do not bother about me at all. I am as happy outside the jail as you are in it." Jawaharlal was instantly contrite and apologetic, even agreeing to replace the defiant statement he had drafted for the court with a cooler piece of legal reasoning prepared by his father. Eventually he was sentenced to thirty months' rigorous imprisonment, but Delhi ordered that the punishment be suspended, and Nehru and his companions were bundled out of the state. The British thought they had triumphed; Jawaharlal saw it differently, and his experience of cooperation with the Akalis led the Congress to assign him party responsibility for Punjab affairs.

At this time Jawaharlal was exercising another function, one which afforded him a great deal of satisfaction. Despite the split with the Swarajists over the Viceroy's Council, the Congress did decide to contest local elections for municipal bodies, and in April 1923 Jawaharlal found himself elected chairman of the Allahabad

Municipal Board. This was a position he did not seek but won because he was the Congressman most acceptable to the city's Muslim councilors, who had rejected the party's official nominee, the traditionalist Congress leader P. D. Tandon. Unprepared for office, Jawaharlal at first grumbled that it would distract him from the national cause, but he soon took to the job and performed creditably, earning a reputation for hard work, incorruptibility, a stubborn management style (with a low threshold of tolerance for inefficiency), and a refusal to play the patronage game. He cut through much of the self-serving cant that surrounded officialdom, refusing to declare a holiday on the anniversary of the Amritsar Massacre because he believed the staff was more interested in a holiday than in mourning the tragedy, and overruling a petty bureaucrat who had denied a prostitute permission to buy a house. ("Prostitutes," he pointed out, "are only one party to the transaction"; if they were obliged to live only in a remote corner of the city, "I would think it equally reasonable to reserve another part of Allahabad for the men who exploit women and because of whom prostitution flourishes.")

But his de facto mayoralty was not only about good civil administration; he unabashedly promoted his nationalist agenda, making Muhammad Iqbal's song "Sare Jahan se Achha Hindustan hamara" ("Better than all the world is our India") a part of the school curriculum, declaring Tilak's death anniversary and the date of Gandhi's sentencing to be public holidays (in lieu of "Empire Day"), and refusing to meet the visiting viceroy, Lord Reading. He even introduced spinning and weaving into the school system. At the same time he had no patience for sectarian causes; he opposed a Hindu member's proposal to ban cow-slaughter, and won the Board's unanimous support. Though Jawaharlal gave up the chairmanship of the municipality after two years in order to devote his energies to national affairs, he missed the job and sought it again in 1928, only to lose that election by a single vote to the pro-Raj "loyalist" candidate.

Political pressures during this period were augmented by personal stress. In November 1924, Kamala gave birth prematurely; her infant son did not survive. Shortly thereafter, her increasingly fragile health took a turn for the worse, and doctors began to suspect tuberculosis. Jawaharlal, repeatedly bedridden with fever, himself underwent a surgical operation in March 1925 for an undisclosed minor ailment. It became clear that he would soon have to take Kamala to Europe for treatment, but he had no money for such an expensive undertaking. Once again Motilal came to the rescue, arranging a legal brief for him with the princely retainer of ten thousand rupees (a sum that Jawaharlal's modest professional experience could not possibly have justified, but which ensured that Motilal himself would keep an eye on the case). It was time, in any case, for a break from the practice of politics; the national movement was not going anywhere, and "as for our politics and public life," Jawaharlal wrote to a friend in November 1925, "I am sick and weary of them." On March 1, 1926, Jawaharlal, Kamala, and the eight-year-old Indira sailed for Europe.

The next twenty months were a hiatus in Nehru's political career but not in the development of his political thought. He boarded his ship in Bombay a committed Gandhian, his worldview shaped almost wholly by the inspirational teachings of the Mahatma. When he returned in December 1927, having spent the interim discovering the intellectual currents of Europe and rethinking his own assumptions, he briefly refused to meet his old mentor. The rebellion was short-lived and did not derive from any fundamental differences over the national question, but it was revealing nonetheless. Jawaharlal left India as Motilal Nehru's son and Mahatma Gandhi's acolyte, but he returned his own man.

It was suggested to him that, in order to facilitate the issuance of a passport for his journey, he provide an assurance that he was not traveling to Europe for political purposes. Even though his primary motive was Kamala's health, which necessitated treatment in Switzerland, Jawaharlal refused to provide any such assurance. The passport was issued anyway; the British had never lost their regard for the Nehrus. His letters to various friends in early 1926 reveal considerable reluctance about his departure, even guilt at being absent from the national political arena; he was anxious about leaving and did not expect to be happy in Europe. Yet by October he was telling his father: "I must confess to a feeling of satisfaction at not being in India just at present. Indeed the whole future outlook is so gloomy that, from the political viewpoint, a return to India is far from agreeable."

Settling initially in inexpensive lodgings in Geneva, Jawaharlal busied himself walking Indira to and from school, nursing Kamala, studying French, managing a prolific correspondence, reading as eclectically as ever, and attending lectures, conferences, and symposia. ("The older I grow the more I feel that there is so much to be learnt and studied and so little time to do it in.") Since Kamala showed little improvement from her treatment, Jawaharlal moved her to a sanatorium in the mountains, at Montana-Vermala in the canton of Valais, near Indira's school at Bex. There he learned skiing and practiced the ice-skating he had learned at Harrow, but he also became restive at his physical and intellectual isolation. It was not long before the Nehrus embarked upon forays into the Continent. Their travels took in Berlin and Heidelberg as well as London and Paris; they visited museums and factories, and Jawaharlal took Indira to Le Bourget to watch, hoisted upon his shoulders, the pioneering aviator Charles Lindbergh land after his historic solo crossing of the Atlantic.

There were, inevitably, dozens of meetings, conversations, and encounters with Indian exiles, students, and revolutionaries, as well as with European political figures. Jawaharlal kept up his writing, publishing a letter in the *Journal de Genève* and numerous articles in the Indian press, one of which, advocating the creation of an "extremist" pressure group in the Congress Party to push for full independence, was interpreted as an attack on the Swarajists and caused Motilal considerable irritation.

But the high point of his political development in Europe came when he was invited to represent the Congress Party at the Brussels International Congress against Colonial Oppression and Imperialism in February 1927. A gathering largely of Soviet sympathizers and "fellow-travelers" (the principal organizer, Willi Muenzenberg, was the man who had coined the phrase), with Communists, pacifists, trade unionists, and nationalists from Africa, Asia, and Latin America as well as Europe, the meeting was clearly aimed at rallying international opposition to imperialism, especially of the British variety. Though the conference was riddled with spies and provocateurs of all stripes (including several secret agents busy double- and triple-crossing each other), Jawaharlal was an active and visible participant, presiding over one of the sessions and drafting many of the resolutions. The Brussels Congress confirmed his conversion to socialism.

The participants' list was a veritable who's who of Europe's leading socialists and Marxists, including Englishmen like the Labourite Fenner Brockway and the leader of the British Communist Party, Harry Pollitt. Nehru was receptive to their ideas. His public statements and speeches explicated his understanding of the forces that sustained imperialism, which drew more deeply from Marxist critiques than previously, including the link between imperialism and capitalism. His resolution on India called not only for independence but for "the full emancipation of the peasants and workers of India, without which there can be no real freedom." He made common cause with the Chinese delegation, drafting a joint Indian-Chinese declaration that hailed three thousand years of cultural links between the two peoples and pledged to work together to thwart British imperialist designs in both countries. (His admiration for China was deeply rooted in a sense of civilizational commonality, and would last through the Communist Revolution, foundering finally on the Himalayan wastes captured by the People's Liberation Army in their war with India in 1962.)

Nehru was the star of the show, his role being crowned by appointment as honorary president of the new body set up by the meeting, the League against Imperialism and for National Independence. Its executive committee included such luminaries as Albert Einstein, the French philosopher and writer Romain Rolland, Madame Sun Yat-sen, the former Labour minister George Lansbury — and Jawaharlal Nehru. Motilal's son had arrived on the international stage.

Father joined son in Europe soon after and was distinctly unenthusiastic about Jawaharlal's keenness to accept an invitation to visit the Soviet Union on the occasion of the tenth anniversary of the 1917 Revolution. In the end Motilal gave in, though he was unamused by the charmlessness of socialist hospitality and the privations the family had to endure in spartan Moscow. Jawaharlal was considerably more impressed with the achievements of the Russian Revolution in "this strange Eurasian country of the hammer and sickle, where workers and peasants sit on the thrones of the mighty and upset the best-laid schemes of mice and men." His four-day visit, supplemented by extensive reading about Russia in English, prompted a series of articles on the USSR in the Indian papers, which were compiled in one volume in December 1928 under the unimaginative title *Soviet Russia: Some Random Sketches and Impressions*. The USSR's progress in such diverse areas as agriculture and literacy, its eradication of class and gender discrimination, its treatment of minorities, and the combination of professionalism and zeal that marked the Leninist revolutionaries, all made a deeply positive impression on the Indian nationalist. Jawaharlal Nehru's first book was, therefore, a paean in praise of the Soviet Union.

Within a year of his return to India he told an audience of students that "though personally I do not agree with many of the methods of [the] communists, and I am by no means sure to what extent communism can suit present conditions in India, I do believe in communism as an ideal of society. For essentially it is socialism, and socialism, I think, is the only way if the world is to escape disaster." In his 1941 book *Towards Freedom*, he wrote that "the theory and philosophy of Marxism lightened up many a dark corner of my mind. . . . I was filled with a new excitement." Such statements would later lead some to see Nehru as a fellow-traveler himself, but the critics overlooked his independence of mind, always his most attractive feature. In a secret report on the International Congress to his own party back in India, Jawaharlal suggested that "the Russians will try to utilize the League to further their own ends," adding: "Personally I have the strongest objection to being led by the nose by the Russians or anybody else."

This capacity for independent thought was confirmed during his European sojourn. The British Labourites who met and patronized him expected his gratitude or at the very least his socialist solidarity, but Nehru saw them as fundamentally in the imperialist camp; he described them in 1928 as "the sanctimonious and canting humbugs who lead the Labour Party." His insights into world affairs revealed both intelligence and acuity. He wrote in 1927 (!) that "England, in order to save herself from extinction, will become a satellite of the United States and incite the imperialism and capitalism of America to fight by her side." He suggested that a Communist victory in China would not necessarily mean that the country would be ruled by the principles of Marx; the role of the "small peasant" would ensure a departure from "pure communism." At the same time he found it difficult to escape the prism of the anticolonial freedom fighter; while taking a benign view of Russian and Chinese communism, he thought that "the great problem of the near future will be American imperialism, even more than British imperialism. Or it may be . . . that the two will join together to create a powerful Anglo-Saxon bloc to dominate the world."

Internationalism was Jawaharlal's forte among Indian nationalist politicians. "I welcome all legitimate methods of getting into touch with other countries and peoples so that we may be able to understand their viewpoint and world politics generally," he wrote to Mahatma Gandhi from Europe in April 1927. "I do not think it is desirable . . . for India to plough a lonely furrow now or in the future. It is solely with a view to self-education and self-improvement that I desire external contacts. I am afraid we are terribly narrow in our outlook and the sooner we get out of this narrowness the better." His broad-mindedness, foreign travels and contacts, and astute judgment of the world situation meant that Jawaharlal had no serious rivals within the Congress Party on international questions. Gandhi, whose own concerns were primarily domestic, was content to leave the field of foreign affairs entirely to his protégé.

It was a physically and intellectually rejuvenated Jawaharlal Nehru who stepped off a ship in Madras in December 1927, just in time to attend the annual session of the Congress which was being held in the southern port city. Motilal had suggested to Gandhi that his son be offered the presidency of the party at the session, but Jawaharlal had turned down an exploratory inquiry from the Mahatma while he was in Switzerland, and Gandhi was reluctant to make the offer anyway: "He is too high-souled to stand the anarchy and hooliganism that seem to be growing in the Congress." Jawaharlal himself took another view in a letter to his close friend Syed Mahmud: "The real objection to me is not youth or jealousy but fear of my radical ideas. I do not propose to tone down my ideas for the presidentship."

But the formerly uncritical Gandhian had returned a self-consciously radical anti-imperialist, impatient with the cautiousness of his elders and convinced that the British connection had to be completely severed. No sooner had the Congress session begun than Jawaharlal was embroiled in a controversy over a draft resolution he submitted calling, in explicit detail, for complete independence for India. The party leaders, including Gandhi himself, thought this was going too far; freedom within the Empire, or Dominion status, was the most they felt they could stake a claim for, and it was already more than the British had shown any inclination to grant. (The British refusal to reciprocate the cooperation extended them by the Indian-elected members of the Viceroy's

Council had already disillusioned both Jinnah and Motilal.) The party elders could not persuade Jawaharlal to back down, however, and a compromise was eventually struck on a demand for "complete national independence," the details left carefully undefined. Most of the radical language in Jawaharlal's draft (calling, for instance, for the immediate withdrawal of Britain's "army of occupation") was excised.

Mahatma Gandhi had not been present in Madras when the resolution was carried, but he wrote in his magazine *Young India* that the resolution was "hastily conceived and thoughtlessly passed" by a Congress descending to the level of a "schoolboys' debating society." Gandhi rebuked Nehru for his zeal, pointing out that "the Congress stultified itself" by passing such resolutions "when it knows that it is not capable of carrying them into effect. By passing such resolutions we make an exhibition of our impotence." These were harsh words; Jawaharlal was furious, and dashed off an excoriating letter to his mentor which so hurt the older man that he destroyed it. A second letter, still angry but more measured, has survived. In it Nehru reiterates his long-held admiration for the Mahatma and expresses his disappointment: "I have asked you many times what you expected to do in the future and your answers have been far from satisfying." That blunt sentence was followed by a long list of objections to the Mahatma's views on matters ranging from religion to contraception. Jawaharlal seemed conscious that his words would cause deep offense. "I have already exceeded all reasonable limits," he wrote in conclusion, acknowledging how far he had strayed from his previously undiluted fealty to the Mahatma. "My only excuse is my mental agitation."

Gandhi's reply saw this as "an open warfare against me and my views. . . . The differences between you and me appear to me to be so vast and radical that there seems to be no meeting ground between us." He made it clear he was prepared to break publicly with his former acolyte, offering to make this correspondence public. Jawaharlal immediately realized he had gone too far. Matters had not been helped by distorted (and sometimes deliberately false) reports in the newspapers suggesting he had been even far more critical in public of Gandhi (one report alleged that he had described the Mahatma as "effete and fossilized"). He wrote an abject letter of apology to "my dear Bapuji" (a term he had begun using for Gandhi, connoting filial devotion): "Am I not your child in politics, though perhaps a truant and errant child?" The Mahatma was disarmed, and immediately forgiving. The crisis between mentor and protégé was defused.

In reality the only difference between their approaches related to timing. Gandhi did not disagree about the ultimate goal, but he believed his countrymen had to be prepared for it through a mass mobilization that had not yet occurred. Jawaharlal's resolution was the work of a few English-educated elitists; it was carried by the party but had not yet aroused the consciousness of the nation. In March 1928 he wrote a letter to the press calling on people who were in favor of independence, against religion in political life, and sought to end class inequalities to get in touch with each other and with him. Nehru himself started two policy study groups within the party to press his agenda — the Republican Congress and the Independence for India League, the latter adding socialism to its republican ideals. But these were again the forums of the privileged. Gandhi wanted to take the issue of freedom beyond the party conclaves, to the people at large. And in doing so he wanted Jawaharlal Nehru by his side.

4

"Hope to Survive the British Empire": 1928–1931

In 1927, while Jawaharlal Nehru was in Europe, the British delivered themselves of an imperial specialty, the insult dressed up as a concession. An all-party commission, the government declared, would be established to visit India and examine whether the country was ready for further constitutional reform. But — and here lay the insult — it would be composed entirely of British members of Parliament. Indian opinion, of all shades, was outraged; though Indians were divided over such issues as political participation and noncooperation, full independence or Dominion status, they were united in their utter rejection of this British offer. Even Liberals like Sir Tej Bahadur Sapru, a loyalist known as Britain's favorite Indian politician, could not swallow the humiliation and refused to have anything to do with the commission.

When Sir John Simon and his six fellow commissioners landed in Bombay on February 3, 1928, they found themselves facing a full-fledged boycott. Thousands of demonstrators thronged the port area holding black flags and placards that echoed their chant: "Simon go back!" Wherever the commission traveled, similar demonstrations took place, often ending in police firing and *lathi*-charges on the unarmed protestors (a *lathi* is a bamboo stave, wielded to great effect by Indian policemen). The visit was an unmitigated fiasco.

Among the principal organizers of the boycott, in his capacity as general secretary of the Congress Party, was Jawaharlal Nehru. When he arrived in Lucknow on November 25, 1928 to rally his followers against the commission's visit to U.P., the national mood had turned particularly ugly, for the Punjab Congress leader Lala Lajpat Rai, a veteran Extremist, had succumbed the previous week to injuries inflicted by the police during his participation in the Lahore protests against Simon. The protest demonstrations in Lucknow were unprecedented in their size and intensity, and demonstrators were twice attacked by the police, with Jawaharlal himself receiving two blows from police batons. When the commission arrived in the city on November 30, the police resorted to a cavalry charge against the demonstrators, beating and trampling hundreds of them; once again, Jawaharlal received several blows from police *lathis*, "a tremendous hammering," in his own words. Public opinion around the country was outraged, and Nehru saw parallels to the country's response to that earlier episode of British brutality, the Amritsar Massacre. "That awakening shook the fabric of British rule," he wrote. "[This] is likely to lead to an even greater national response which may carry us to our goal."

The Simon Commission had succeeded in giving a greater impetus to political change in India than its creators had intended. It had galvanized the nation and united it in a common cause. And it had helped anoint a new national hero. Jawaharlal had been "half-blinded with the blows" but had had enough presence of mind to refuse the offer of two revolvers from a police agent seeking to entrap him in the midst of the melée. The grace under pressure he revealed on that occasion was also reflected in a telegram he sent anxious friends in London: "Thanks. Injuries severe but not serious. Hope [to] survive the British Empire." The Mahatma was warm in his admiration. "It was all done bravely. You have braver things to do. May God spare you for many a long year to come and make you His chosen instrument for freeing India from the yoke."

How the yoke was to be lifted, though, remained unclear. The British had suggested that Indians were only capable of obstructive opposition but could not come up with any constitutional proposals of their own. Responding to the challenge, the Congress set up a committee in 1928 under Motilal Nehru to propose a Constitution for free India. The resulting document, known to the public as the Nehru Report, had a wide degree of backing from various sections of Indian opinion for a democratic Indian Dominion within the British Empire. But Jinnah opposed it bitterly, denouncing it as a "Hindu report" even as most of his fellow Muslim League leaders endorsed the document. Jinnah's anger was principally due to Motilal's rejection of separate electorates for different religious groups, a point he had discussed with Jinnah's close aide M. C. Chagla while Jinnah was absent in Europe. Motilal had been willing to agree upon separate electorates, but it was Chagla, a liberal Muslim (and later a distinguished jurist, diplomat, and cabinet minister in free India), who had pointed out that such a provision would undermine national unity and had no place in the constitution of a free India. Jinnah's opposition destroyed the prospects of the Motilal Nehru Report forming the basis of a structure of governance for a united and independent India (and precipitated a permanent break between Jinnah and the brilliant and broad-minded Chagla). Ironically, Motilal's own son had felt that, in its willingness to settle for Dominion status, it did not go far enough in the direction of full independence. Motilal, elected president of the Congress Party at its Calcutta session in 1928, did not mind: "Jawahar would not be my son if he did not stick to his guns."

And yet his guns were never quite primed to be fired. "It is obvious," Jawaharlal wrote to a leftist Muslim friend in September 1928, "that the Congress contains at least two if not more groups which have nothing in common between them and the sooner they break apart the better." But he did nothing to bring about such a break, conscious as he undoubtedly was that any rupture would find his own father and his mentor, the Mahatma, on the opposite side of the ideological divide. With Jawaharlal Nehru, principle would always be tempered by loyalty, conviction moderated by custom. (His great contemporary and rival Netaji Subhas Chandra Bose spoke dismissively of Nehru's "sentimental politics.") Jawaharlal was always willing to express a radical view — twice that year coming close to arrest for his utterances alone — but the ardent revolutionary in him invariably gave way to the conciliator, seeking common ground with those he admired and whom he would not, indeed could not, betray. To that extent he was Motilal's son: his father had told him bluntly that "pure idealism divorced from realities has no place in politics."

That common ground was found not on the issue of principle but on that of timing. Jawaharlal and Gandhi both found it possible to agree on the Nehru Report as the Congress Party's immediate demand; if the British government did not implement its demands within two years, the Mahatma declared, the Congress would shift to its long-term goal of full independence. Jawaharlal thought two years too long, and the Mahatma obligingly cut the deadline back to one year. The younger Nehru accepted the compromise but, to reaffirm his principles, stayed away from the session of the Congress that adopted it. Gandhi praised him publicly for swallowing his dissatisfaction: "a high-souled man as he is, he does not want to create unnecessary bitterness. . . . He would not be Jawaharlal if he did not strike out for himself an absolutely unique and original line in pursuance of his path. He considers nobody, not even his father . . . [only] his duty to his own country."

Since neither man seriously believed that the British government would adopt the Nehru Report within anything like a year, Jawaharlal spent 1929 as the party's general secretary preparing himself for the confrontation he was sure would follow. At Gandhi's urging, he traveled throughout the country organizing and reviving the local units of the party. Unimpressed by the far from businesslike way in which they conducted their work, he poured a great deal of energy (and much of his own money, which was hardly plentiful) into the party organization. He paid particular attention to creating teams of volunteers, who in turn were to raise the consciousness of workers and peasants about the coming struggle for freedom. Jawaharlal was also president, though not a very active one, of the All-India Trade Union Congress, seeking to rally organized labor to the nationalist cause. The British government regarded his activities with growing concern; the Home Secretary wrote to his subordinates in the provinces that "[t]here is a tendency for the political and the Communist revolutionaries to join hands, and Pandit Jawaharlal Nehru, an extreme nationalist who is at the same time genuinely attracted by some of the Communist doctrines, stands at about the meeting point."

Seeking to drive a wedge between the Communists and the nationalists, the British prosecuted thirty-one Communist leaders at Meerut in April 1929, and the Congress chose to defend them. The trial dragged on for three and a half years. It was widely expected that Jawaharlal himself would be arrested and prosecuted on the same grounds, but though some of his statements were cited, and a forged letter attributed to the Indian Communist M. N. Roy was produced which purported to describe Jawaharlal as a "liaison agent" with the Soviets, the British concluded they did not have enough credible evidence to support the charge that he was a Communist. In fact the Communist leader Muzaffar Ahmed privately thought of Jawaharlal as a "timid reformist." Indian and foreign Communists saw him as one who uttered Communist slogans but took no steps to achieve them; his rhetoric, they argued, aimed not at revolution but at "getting support from the proletariat" for his nationalist goals. Yet the threat of arrest did have one positive result. It prompted Jawaharlal to give up smoking in preparation for jail, a decision with long-term benefits for his health (though subsequent lapses were not unknown).

In the meantime Gandhi began preparing the ground for a political earthquake: he wanted Motilal to be succeeded as president of the Congress Party by his son. Jawaharlal was reluctant, pleading with the Mahatma that his "personal inclination always is not to be shackled down to any office. I prefer to be free and to have the time to act according to my own inclinations." He was also conscious that he would not be the genuinely democratic choice of the party; any support he got, he argued, would largely be aimed at keeping others out. But Gandhi would not be deterred. He cajoled and cudgeled Jawaharlal into submission, overcoming the objections even of Motilal himself, who feared that imposing his son on the party would not be fair either to the party or to Jawaharlal. (Ironically, it was Motilal who had first suggested to the Mahatma that "the need of the hour is the head of Gandhi and the voice of Jawahar.") Sardar Vallabhbhai Patel, fifteen years older than

Jawaharlal and a doughty organizer who was already being thought of as the "Iron Man" of the Congress, had more support than Nehru for the top job. But though the All-India Congress Committee (AICC) was not enthusiastic about Gandhi's announcement that Jawaharlal would lead it, the party could not repudiate the Mahatma. On September 29, 1929, two months before his fortieth birthday, Jawaharlal Nehru was elected to preside over the Congress at its December session in Lahore.

Though his father's presumptuous notation on that old postcard to Harrow had come true, the election of Jawaharlal as Congress president was hardly the great triumph it has since been portrayed as being. The only one who really sought it was Gandhi, who saw great symbolic value in passing the torch to the embodiment of a new generation — but who simultaneously declared that Jawaharlal was such a faithful acolyte of his that his being president was just as good as the Mahatma himself holding the job. The shrewd Mahatma had no doubt calculated that if he did not publicly co-opt Jawaharlal into the party establishment at the expense of the conservative Patel, the younger Nehru could drift away into active radicalism. Those party elders who reluctantly voted for him did so not out of any great love for Jawaharlal but out of regard for Gandhi; many hoped that the presidency would rein in the younger man's tendency to hotheadedness, keeping the proponents of "full independence" within the Congress tent. Jawaharlal's leftist and "Extremist" allies, though, expected him to use his position to lead the party away from what they saw as the temporizing of the Nehru Report into a full-throated battle for freedom from British rule. Jawaharlal himself, aware of these contrary pulls, accepted the honor with unfeigned diffidence. He wrote to a close friend that it would not be easy in his new assignment "to avoid losing all my cheerfulness and light-heartedness." The perceptive nationalist poet Sarojini Naidu, whose daughter Padmaja was to become an intimate of Nehru's, wrote to Jawaharlal: "I wonder if in the whole of India there [is] a prouder heart than your father's or a heavier heart than yours."

And yet there was no doubt about Jawaharlal's potential as a leader. The Congress politician Y. B. Chavan recounted meeting Jawaharlal at a public gathering around 1929, when he was fifteen and Nehru forty. The impact of the leader on the crowd was inspirational: "The younger ones among us swore by the vigor of his intellect, the freshness of his outlook, and the radiance of his youth; the older folk nodded to one another, wondering at the wise head he carried on his young shoulders; and admiring women agreed with both."

The country was at a crossroads: the Simon Commission's visit had been a disaster; the Nehru Report was looking increasingly like a dead letter; Hindu-Muslim relations had declined from the peak of amity at the beginning of the decade; the cracks in the Congress Party could barely be papered over; and young men were turning to violence. In April 1929 the now legendary Bhagat Singh threw bombs into the Legislative Assembly, expressing the hope that the explosions would "make the deaf hear" (he was hanged for his pains, but in 2002 the popular Indian film industry of Bollywood would release not one but five competing films about his courage and daring). It was widely expected that, with Jawaharlal in the chair and the Mahatma's one-year deadline having expired, the Congress would push for full independence (*purna swaraj*) at its Lahore session in December 1929. Looking for ways to head off the impending crisis, the British viceroy, Lord Irwin, announced on October 31, 1929 that His Majesty's Government would convene, at a date to be determined, a Round Table Conference of all the Indian parties to discuss the country's future. Irwin's declaration included, almost as an afterthought, the admission that "the natural issue of India's constitutional progress . . . is the attainment of Dominion Status." This might have been treated seriously by a Congress still formally committed to the Nehru Report, but Irwin's words created such an outcry from the blimps and the reactionaries in the British Parliament that it vitiated whatever appreciation such an announcement might have elicited from Indian opinion-makers. Irwin himself, scalded by the outrage back home, backpedaled swiftly away from any suggestion that Dominion status was imminent. Gandhi initially responded favorably to the announcement, prompting Jawaharlal to offer his resignation from his party positions; but when the British refused to honor the four provisos the Congress had put forward for its support, the danger of a split in the Congress ranks receded. The singularly unimaginative Irwin did not even offer to release political prisoners, a gesture that would have met one of Gandhi's conditions and helped win the Mahatma's cooperation.

That ended the last hope of compromise on the issue with the Indian National Congress. Two days before the

Congress session, Irwin met with Gandhi and Motilal from the Congress, along with Jinnah, representing the Muslim League, and the Liberals Sapru and V. J. Patel, to urge a more measured pace for change. On a day when a terrorist bomb had exploded under the viceroy's railway carriage, the other three were amenable to seeing things Irwin's way; the Congress leaders were not. The meeting marked the irretrievable breakdown between the Congress and those Indians who were still prepared to work within the British framework. Motilal and the Mahatma traveled to and from the meeting in one vehicle, the three others in a different car. They no longer agreed either on the destination or on how to get there.

On December 25, 1929 the citizens of Lahore greeted the Christmas holiday by turning out in large numbers to hail the new young president of the Congress as he trotted down the narrow thoroughfares on a white steed, resplendent in a long black *sherwani* coat, waving as women sprinkled him with rose petals from the windows. Motilal saw the adulation from his perch on a balcony in the Anarkali marketplace, and was inspired to quote Persian poetry to the effect that the son had surpassed the father. Contemporary accounts describe the excitement now generated by the ascension of the forty-year-old Jawaharlal Nehru to the leadership of the party. Gone were memories of the reluctance with which the party had chosen him; instead his call for *purna swaraj* was unanimously passed, and on the night of December 29 the new president raised the flag of a free India. It was saffron, white, and green, its three horizontal stripes capturing three colors that were sacred to, and touched the hearts of, India's major communities (and which stood, respectively, for courage, unity, and fertility, among other virtues). In the middle was a spinning wheel, proclaiming the country's attachment to self-reliance. Jawaharlal made a stirring speech about the flag standing for all Indians, whether Hindu or Muslim; and as the stars twinkled in an ink-black sky, men and women, President Nehru himself among them, danced with childlike jubilation around the flagpole. It was midnight, but few doubted that a new dawn had broken over India.

"The love for the idea of India," wrote a British conservative in Lahore, "is one of the finest, and also one of the most incalculable, forces in the country." Mahatma Gandhi, who just a year earlier had thought that Jawaharlal had been too hasty in his advocacy of full independence at the Madras session, embraced the new spirit. He proposed that Indians in every village or town across the land observe "Independence Day" on January 26 by taking a pledge to end exploitation, restore liberty, break the chains of their slavery, and resolve to defend themselves without the help of the Raj. "We hold it to be a crime against man and God to submit any longer to [British] rule," declared the pledge. "It is the inalienable right of the Indian people, as of any other people, to have freedom and to enjoy the fruits of their toil." For the next seventeen years, this pledge would be repeated throughout India. January 26 ceased to be "Independence Day" when freedom eventually came at midnight on August 15, 1947; but twenty years after the initial pledge, an independent India would adopt its republican Constitution on January 26, 1950, so that this day of national emotional significance could continue to be celebrated as "Republic Day."

Jawaharlal Nehru's Congress was, to use a contemporary idiom, pushing the envelope as far as it would go, but still the British did not crack down. While Mahatma Gandhi began to prepare for a campaign of civil disobedience to give effect to the independence pledge, Jawaharlal turned his attention to two vital domestic political issues. First, he took on the Communists, denouncing their attempts to infiltrate the Congress as the work of British agents, and condemning their capture of the League against Imperialism and for National Independence, from whose Executive Committee he offered to resign. (He was expelled from it as a "left reformist" in 1931.) Then he addressed the concerns of Muslim Congressmen who feared that Gandhian civil disobedience would simply lead to communal rioting as had been seen in the mid-1920s. Where the Mahatma seemed to believe that the risk could be ignored, Nehru made specific commitments to offer various protections to the minorities. He wanted the Muslim population behind the Congress's campaign.

Then Mahatma Gandhi embarked on the first act of willful lawbreaking that would capture the imagination of the country and the world. To defy a British tax on salt, he led thousands of followers on a 241-mile march from his Sabarmati ashram to the Gujarat seacoast at Dandi, surrounded by the cameras and notebooks of enthralled reporters, and broke the law by letting a raised fistful of seawater evaporate in his hand, leaving an illegal residue of untaxed salt in his palm. Jawaharlal later wrote of the indelible sight of the Mahatma "marching, staff in hand, to Dandi. . . . He was the pilgrim on his quest for truth, quiet, peaceful, determined and fearless." Salt was a commodity every poor Indian needed to consume; by drawing attention to the British salt monopoly, the Mahatma demonstrated the iniquity of imperialism far more effectively than a thousand other protests might have done. "Today the pilgrim marches onwards on his long trek," Jawaharlal wrote at his most poetic. "The fire of a great resolve is in him. . . . And love of truth that scorches and love of freedom that inspires. And none that pass him can escape the spell, and men of common clay feel the spark of life."

As the march progressed, with the government unable to arrest Gandhi until he had actually broken the law, Jawaharlal and other party leaders galvanized popular support for the cause in a nation already transfixed by the media's reporting of the frail Mahatma's political pilgrimage. In a gesture rich with symbolism, Gandhi chose April 6, the anniversary of the Amritsar Massacre, to break the law. The moment the Mahatma held his handful of salt up to the cameras, Jawaharlal led the nation in echoing his act of defiance by collecting salt from the sea and from salt-bearing rocks, in selling contraband salt and in courting arrest for doing so. "Will you be mere lookers-on in this glorious struggle?" he demanded of Indian youth. "What shall it profit you to get your empty degrees and your mess of pottage if the millions starve and your motherland continues in bondage? Who lives if India dies? Who dies if India lives?" His wife, Kamala, despite her frailty, and his sister Krishna ("Betty") joined him in Allahabad's first batch of satyagrahis. On April 14 he was finally taken into custody. "Great Day!" he wrote in his diary as he was thrown into solitary confinement for six months.

But conditions were more severe than in his previous stint in jail — he was, for instance, only allowed to write and receive one letter a week, and was denied daily newspapers — and he did not help matters by refusing special privileges offered to him, such as sweets from his home and the use of a manual fan (*punkah*) operated by a pair of prison servants. Exercise was, however, possible, as was weaving, spinning, and, of course, reading. He devoured Bukharin, Bertrand Russell, and Spengler, read Maurois and Rolland in French, and even threw in Lloyd George's speeches and Shakespeare's sonnets. He was allowed to take notes, though he rarely needed to consult them; once he had finished a book it found a place in his mental reference library.

Nehru's prison diary reveals how he closely followed political events in the outside world — the Peshawar disturbances in April, which showed that an overwhelmingly Muslim population had heeded the call to rise against the British (and featured a remarkable incident in which Hindu soldiers laid down their weapons rather than use them against their Muslim compatriots), episodes of police firing in Calcutta, Madras, and Karachi (three corners of the subcontinent), and the arrest of Mahatma Gandhi on May 5, which confirmed that the British and the Indians were now embarked on a "full-blooded war to the bitter end." Then, on June 30, a new prisoner was brought into his jail: Motilal Nehru. Though the father was clearly ailing and would soon be released on grounds of ill health, by July the two were caught up in political negotiations with the British, the Liberal Sapru acting as a willfully self-deluding mediator. At Sapru's urging the Nehrus were transported in a special train to meet the Mahatma at his prison, Yeravda Central Jail, in August to discuss (despite Jawaharlal's obvious obduracy) the terms of a possible settlement with the British government. In these negotiations it was Jawaharlal's uncompromising view that prevailed. The British secretary of state for India wrote of his unhappiness at "Gandhi's deference to Jawaharlal and Jawaharlal's pride . . . which depressed me, because it did not show the spirit of a beaten man."

Indeed Jawaharlal was anything but beaten. His six-month sentence ended on October 11; within eight days he was back in jail. Resuming his interrupted presidency of the Congress, he had defiantly called for renewed civil disobedience:

> It is clear that India, big as it is, is not big enough to contain both the Indian people and the British Government. One of the two has to go and there can be little doubt as to which. . . . [W]e are in deadly earnest, we have burnt our boats . . . and there is no going back for us.

In his case there was a "going back" — to prison, this time for sedition and for a much longer term of two years' rigorous imprisonment, with an additional five months if he did not pay his five-hundred-rupee fine, which of course he had no intention of doing.

During his brief period of liberty (memorialized, typically, in a pamphlet he authored called *The Eight-Day Interlude*) Jawaharlal had visited his ailing father at the hill station of Mussoorie. Motilal, who had taken over his jailed son's presidency as Jawaharlal's nominated replacement when Mahatma Gandhi was arrested, called for Indians to celebrate his son's forty-first birthday as "Jawahar Day." The occasion was marked by anti-British demonstrations around the country (and in Colombo) involving more than twenty million demonstrators; twenty people lost their lives to police bullets and another fifteen hundred were wounded. Recording the events in his prison diary, Jawaharlal allowed his exhilaration to outweigh his sadness. It seemed as if battle had truly been joined.

"If Jawahar lives for ten years," Motilal wrote to a nephew in 1928, "he will change the face of India." But he added: "Such men do not usually live long; they are consumed by the fire within them." The father's fears proved unfounded; Jawaharlal had another thirty-six years to live. Instead it was Motilal whom destiny had chosen for a rapid demise. The years of political agitation and imprisonment had taken a devastating toll on the formerly sybaritic lawyer; his chronic asthma was now a daily trial, there was fibrosis in his lungs and a tumor in his chest. When, in January 1931, he came to see his son in prison on the one family visit permitted Jawaharlal every fortnight, Motilal could barely speak; even his mind seemed to wander. It was clear to the son that only his father's indomitable will was keeping him going.

On January 26 Jawaharlal was released by the British to go to his father's deathbed. Early on February 6, after a restless and tormented night, the end came. In the son's words: "his face grew calm and the sense of struggle vanished from it." Motilal's last words on earth were to Mahatma Gandhi, in praise of the Garhwalis, the Hindu troops who had refused to fire on the Muslim Khudai Khidmatgar protestors in Peshawar the previous year. It was entirely appropriate that his last living thought should have been for Hindu-Muslim unity in India. The old Khilafat campaigner Muhammad Ali had once declared that the only Hindus trusted by all Muslims were Gandhi and the two Nehrus. Now there was only one Nehru left; Jawaharlal would have to shoulder Motilal's share of the anticommunal burden.

Motilal's influence on his son, and by extension on the fortunes of India, cannot be underestimated. (Motilal's love of India, Mahatma Gandhi once said, was derived from his love of Jawaharlal, and not the other way around.) It was Motilal's liberal and rationalist temperament that gave Jawaharlal his scientific inclinations and his agnosticism; the Motilal who defied Hindu orthodoxy by traveling abroad was the progenitor of the Jawaharlal who had little time for the priesthood or the self-appointed guardians of any faith. Motilal's abhorrence of bigotry, his contempt for the Hindu communalists who mirrored the Muslim League with their sectarian Hindu Mahasabha, found echoes in his son. Jawaharlal was ideologically the more radical — Motilal would never have called himself a socialist — but he imbibed from his father's sturdy moderation a capacity for compromise that enabled him repeatedly to find common ground with his party's old guard. Above all it was

Motilal's unshakable faith in his son's greatness that gave Jawaharlal the aura of self-confidence that marks so many of the major figures of history. His father saw a man of destiny in Jawaharlal well before anyone else could spot any but the most modest qualities in his son. Motilal's formidable will, and his hands-on mentoring, had helped bring Jawaharlal to this point. Now he was on his own.

In turn Jawaharlal sought to instill in his only child something comparable to what Motilal had done for his only son. He had written sporadically to the young Indira since she was five, but during his imprisonment in 1930 he consciously sought to make up for his absence as a father by educating her through his letters. Jawaharlal's wide and eclectic reading, his notes, and his own remarkable mind had to compensate for the lack of a shelf of reference books, as he embarked on a series of letters intended to outline for Indira his vision of the history of humankind. Raleigh and Condorcet had written comparable works during their incarcerations, but there was no Indian precedent for this extraordinary endeavor. Starting with the roots of ancient Indian civilization in Mohenjodaro, taking in ancient Greece and Rome, and traveling through China and the Arab world before coming to the triumph of European imperialism in the nineteenth and early twentieth centuries, the letters are a remarkable testament to Jawaharlal Nehru's intellect and his sense of humanity. Written over three years in jail without research assistance of any kind and published in one volume under the title *Glimpses of World History*, the letters transcended their stated purpose to stand for something rarely seen in the political world — the revelation of the insights into human history that inspired the worldview of an uncommon statesman.

The letters were too much for the poorly educated Indira; she read them sporadically if at all, and it soon became clear that they were meant for a larger audience than the daughter to whom they were addressed. On New Year's Day 1931 her mother was arrested for leading a women's demonstration; typically the news of Kamala's arrest (and especially of her defiant statement as she was carted off to jail, saying, "I am happy beyond measure and proud to follow in the footsteps of my husband") delighted Jawaharlal, who completely overlooked the fact that it would leave a thirteen-year-old at home without either parent at a time when the larger family was consumed with the condition of her dying grandfather. Motilal's letters to his son were full of practical advice, paternal love and pride, friendly reassurance (and some political observations); Jawaharlal's cerebral ones to his daughter were completely removed from the quotidian concerns of her lonely life. If Motilal left his stamp on Jawaharlal by being a fully engaged and even overdirective father, Jawaharlal's influence on Indira would be marked by his disengagement from her needs.

While Motilal lay dying, however, the British sought compromise. They had convened a Round Table Conference while the Congress leaders were in jail and realized it was an exercise in futility; for a second round to succeed in bringing peace to the country, they had to treat with Gandhi and his followers. The Labour government of Ramsay MacDonald released the prisoners (as it happened, on January 26) and suggested the terms of a compromise leading to fundamental constitutional reforms. Jawaharlal was deeply suspicious about the offer ("the British Government are past masters in the art of political chicanery and fraud, and we are babes at their game") and urged its rejection. He did not accept the notion that Labourites were more sympathetic to India: "Almost every Englishman, however advanced he may be politically, is a bit of an imperialist in matters relating to India." But, shell-shocked by his father's painful descent into death, he proved unable to rally the other party leaders or to persuade the Mahatma to see it his way. Negotiations with the viceroy were entrusted to Gandhi (who, on being told that Lord Irwin always prayed to God before making any major decision, once remarked, "what a pity God gives him such bad advice"). In London, the bombastic imperialist Winston Churchill growled his dismay at the "nauseating" sight of "a seditious Middle Temple lawyer . . . striding half-naked up the steps of the Viceregal palace . . . to parley on equal terms with the representative of the King-Emperor." (Churchill rather undermined his impact by describing the Mahatma in the same statement as a "fakir of a type well known in the East." On Indian subjects his racism usually got the better of his judgment: a fakir is a religious Muslim mendicant and the Gandhian "type" was hardly well known except for the Mahatma himself.)

But this time the reactionaries in London would not be allowed by the British government to scuttle compromise in New Delhi. In talks that riveted the national and world press, Gandhi met with the viceroy between

February 17 and March 4 and, after eight sessions adding up to over twenty-four hours of intense give-and-take, signed an agreement that would become known to history as the Gandhi-Irwin Pact. Under the pact, to Jawaharlal's dismay, the Mahatma agreed to take part in a second Round Table Conference in London in exchange for the release of political prisoners and for permission to picket and protest nonviolently. Jawaharlal thought these terms were humiliating and — still mourning the loss of his father — hurtfully told Gandhi that had Motilal been alive he would have negotiated a better deal. But the die was cast. The Mahatma threatened to retire from politics if his agreement was repudiated by the Congress.

As so often happened, Jawaharlal gave in and actually proposed the resolution at the Karachi Congress in March 1931 ratifying Gandhi's terms. He made no secret of his objections but, unlike in 1929, did not even offer to resign, urging all Congressmen to put aside their differences and follow the directions of the party's Working Committee. The British had feared he might split the party and lead a radical group into continued civil disobedience, but (as when they thought he was a Communist) they had failed to understand Motilal Nehru's son. "We cannot afford to get excited in politics," Jawaharlal advised a young party worker in 1931. "We must preserve our balance and not rush into any action without proper consideration. . . . [We must not] lose the benefit of collective action and of [a united] organization."

Once again, Jawaharlal chose to bide his time. He had lost a father, but in the Mahatma he had a father figure whom he could not betray. If Gandhi thought his pact and a Round Table Conference were tactically the right means to the ultimate end of Indian freedom, Jawaharlal was prepared to swallow his objections, however profound his disagreement. In any case, the nation was with the Mahatma, and Gandhi did not disagree with him over the eventual goal. When the viceroy and the Mahatma toasted their pact over a cup of tea, Gandhi mischievously produced some contraband salt from under his shawl. "I will put some of this salt into my tea," he announced, "to remind us of the famous Boston Tea-Party." The viceroy was gracious enough to laugh, but neither man needed reminding that, in less than a decade after that event, the American colonists were free of their British rulers.

5

"In Office but Not in Power": 1931–1937

In concluding the Gandhi-Irwin Pact the viceroy disregarded one of the Mahatma's pleas, that the lives of the young revolutionary Bhagat Singh and his companions, who had been arrested for throwing bombs into the Legislative Assembly, be spared. Less than three weeks after the agreement, on March 23, the patriots were hanged; angry demonstrators blamed Gandhi's pact with the British for their deaths. Jawaharlal himself declared that "the corpse of Bhagat Singh shall stand between us and England." But Sardar Vallabhbhai Patel, who had succeeded him as Congress president, aided the Mahatma in steering the party's Karachi session toward moderation. Nehru's major contribution at Karachi was the formulation of a "minimum program" for the Congress, which guaranteed Indians freedom of expression and assembly, equality before the law, universal adult franchise, and a secular state, as well as a number of less easily realizable social and economic rights. The resolution embodying these freedoms passed after some resistance from the right wing, and went on to constitute the nucleus of the Constitution that free India would give itself nearly two decades later.

After a break holidaying in Ceylon with Kamala and Indira for seven weeks, an all-too-rare gesture of attention to his neglected family, Jawaharlal returned to political action. Seeing the unrest amongst the U.P. peasantry, long oppressed by their British-imposed landlords, or *taluqdars*, he decided to launch a campaign against the payment of rent. He was careful not to do this as a form of class warfare, instead couching his appeals in anti-British terms, since the government clearly had the capacity to provide relief to the tenant farmers but chose not to do so. Ordered by the government to discontinue his public speaking in favor of the "no-rent" campaign, Jawaharlal refused. He was arrested on December 26, 1931 and, early in the New Year, sentenced to the usual two years' rigorous imprisonment and a five-hundred-rupee fine. (Once again he refused to pay the fine, and the authorities seized a car registered in Indira's name, which they subsequently auctioned off for three times the amount of the fine.)

The struggle was already requiring him to draw upon inner resources he had not known he possessed. His sister Vijayalakshmi Pandit would never forget Jawaharlal's imprisonment this time:

> We were permitted to go and say good-bye. He was his usual self, full of assurances . . . and humorous

> messages to the younger members of the family. As we walked away, I turned back for a last look. He stood against the sun which was setting in a great orange ball behind his head. He held the bars on either side and the face, so recently full of mirth, was serene and withdrawn, and there was infinite compassion in the eyes, which no longer saw us. He was already deep in his own contemplation.

Mahatma Gandhi was at sea, literally and metaphorically, at the time of Jawaharlal's arrest. He was returning from the second Round Table Conference, which had proved as infructuous as the first, when the news reached him on board his ship from London. The Conservatives had returned to power in Britain and London was no longer enthused by Irwin's conciliatory approach. Irwin's successor, the disagreeable Tory grandee Lord Willingdon, did not consider it part of a viceroy's brief to mollify law-breaking Indians; indeed he saw himself as "a sort of Mussolini in India." Under Willingdon the British adopted a general policy of political repression, banning the Congress, seizing its properties, confiscating its assets, destroying its records, and prohibiting political activity. The press was censored and thousands of "subversives" were jailed, among them Jawaharlal, seen as a potential Indian Lenin. He spent most of the next four years in prison, with only two brief spells of freedom.

During the first of these stints behind bars, beginning just after Christmas 1931, his health suffered; unexplained fevers, tooth ailments, and a bout of pleurisy laid him low, and he was unable to maintain his regular exercise. (Later, he mastered yoga and wrote of "standing on his head" in his prison cell.) Conditions were abominable, with bedbugs, mosquitoes, flies, wasps, and even bats his constant companions. The fortnightly visits from his relatives were so closely monitored, and his visitors so badly treated, that he placed a self-imposed ban on them rather than see his family insulted — but not seeing his family only heightened his anxiety about their welfare. (The Mahatma finally persuaded him to end this self-denial after eight months.) In April 1932 his mother was badly beaten about the head and severely injured when a demonstration she was participating in was *lathi*-charged by the police. "The mother of a brave son is also somewhat like him," she wrote, but Jawaharlal's despondency was great — a chronically ill wife, a neglected daughter, and now a widowed mother who had nearly died at the hands of the police, in addition to his two sisters also being jailed, all weighed on him. There is a photograph of him in prison at this time, nearly bald, attired in a white dhoti (full-length waistcloth) and kurta (loose-fitting shirt) with a black khadi (homespun) waistcoat buttoned above the navel. He is posing for the camera with his hands behind his back, but there is no hiding the grim pallor of his countenance, the downturned cast of his mouth, the hollowness of the determined expression he has put on. This is a man living in the depths. A year before, he had been dancing around the flagpole in Lahore.

His only consolation in prison lay in his continued writing of the letters to Indira on world history — letters that he was not, for a while, allowed to send her. They reveal Jawaharlal's vision of human progress, advancing through periods of inhumanity and suffering but teleologically moving onward toward better lives for the world's ordinary people. The Marxian idea that control of the means of production is the key to political dominance, and that history is essentially a tale of class conflict, strongly informs his analysis. But his British liberal education also shows through, as does his syncretic view of Indian nationalism. Jawaharlal was certainly aware that his letters would find a larger public, and in writing about India as well as the world he was careful to articulate views consistent with his political objectives. There is great praise for the Indian epics the Ramayana and the Mahabharata (in particular the Bhagavad Gita), but as works of literature rather than as sacred texts; and he is careful to write about Islam with respect, describing even the depredations of the eleventh-century invader Mahmud of Ghazni as nothing more than the deeds of a warrior of those times rather than as evidence of what Hindu chauvinists were portraying as Muslim barbarism. In these letters there clearly emerge the fundamental convictions of the young statesman: his secularism, his socialism (underscored by the seeming collapse of capitalism with the global depression then at its worst), his detestation of strongmen (linked to the rise of fascism in Europe, which he believed only communism could defeat), and his faith in a "scientific" approach to human history.

Though writing (and eclectic reading, this time without restrictions) warded off some of the tedium of jail, Jawaharlal spent a great deal of his solitude mourning his father. On one occasion he was reading a newspaper article about the unveiling of a bust of Motilal when he suddenly found his eyes full of tears. He had always known how much he was reliant on that strong, protective, and overindulgent paternal force in his life, and he was now suffused with the extent of his loss. The Mahatma was, of course, the closest substitute. When Gandhi undertook a fast-unto-death in September 1932 in protest against a British decision to treat the "Untouchables" as a separate community outside the Hindu fold, Jawaharlal feared he would lose a second father figure. (Gandhi, who had been seeking to reform the discriminatory practices within Hinduism in order to ensure the Untouchables — whom he called Harijans, or "Children of God" — full acceptance within Hindu society, saw the British decision as a further scheme to divide Indians against each other.) That crisis passed, but in 1933 Gandhi undertook another potentially fatal fast and an anxious Jawaharlal cabled him: "I feel lost in a strange country where you are [the] only familiar landmark and I try to grope my way in [the] dark but I stumble." Yet politically the two diverged more and more; Jawaharlal's prison diaries reveal his increasing conviction that Gandhi was too willing to compromise with reactionary social, political, and religious forces which were anathema to the radical Nehru. The Mahatma derived his ethic from God; the author of *Glimpses of World History* derived his from Man, or at least from his study of mankind. He found Gandhi's "frequent references to God . . . most irritating."

On August 12, 1933, with his mother seriously ill and his sentence having less than two weeks to run, the British released Jawaharlal. Perhaps they expected him to break decisively with Gandhi and split the Congress Party. Indeed, Jawaharlal traveled to Poona to meet the Mahatma in a somewhat rebellious mood. But once again the two men found common ground; his great need for the paternal figure of Gandhi, his admiration for the Mahatma's common touch with ordinary Indians (which he, as an aristocratic intellectual, felt he could never match), and his conviction that party unity was indispensable for an effective freedom struggle, prompted Jawaharlal to articulate his views in terms that the Mahatma could live with. Gandhi declared the differences between them to be merely those of temperament; he told an interviewer that Jawaharlal's "communist views . . . need not frighten anyone." Some of Nehru's radical followers in the Congress were disappointed at this seeming gulf between analysis and action, but it was wholly characteristic of Jawaharlal. Rather than attacking the Congress leadership, he turned his anger against the forces of Hindu bigotry which had begun to organize themselves under the Hindu Mahasabha. (In an approach that would lead to him being forever accused of double standards, he was less harsh on Muslim communalism, seeing this as to some degree excusable in a minority afraid for its future.)

Nonetheless his new pact with Gandhi made him a dangerous figure in British eyes. The authorities feared the pair would shortly revive the dormant civil disobedience movement, this time with a communistic tinge. The government sent secret instructions around the country that Jawaharlal was to be closely watched, and arrested at the slightest provocation. Various speeches were examined as suitable candidates for prosecution, before a stinging denunciation of imperialism in Calcutta in January 1934 gave the Bengal government the excuse to arrest and try him. In February he was sentenced to another two years in His Majesty's prisons.

After three months with no books other than a German grammar, no companion other than a clerk jailed for embezzlement, and severe restrictions on his writing, Jawaharlal was transferred from Calcutta to a prison in the U.P. hills, in Dehra Dun. In April a disillusioned Mahatma Gandhi suspended civil disobedience altogether, to Jawaharlal's great disappointment. Yet again, Jawaharlal confided to his diary that the time had come for a parting of the ways with his mentor. "I felt with a stab of pain that the cords of allegiance that had bound me to him for many years had snapped." He said as much in an emotional letter to Gandhi, which the Mahatma chose to regard merely as the letting off of steam rather than the sign of a definitive break. Gandhi was wise: Jawaharlal had no taste for patricide. Briefly released from prison on compassionate grounds — Kamala's health was worsening by the day — he disassociated himself from public criticism of the Congress leaders, to the dismay of his leftist followers, who had constituted themselves into a Congress Socialist Party and were looking to him for leadership. Jawaharlal kept his disagreements with Gandhi to himself; in any case the British authorities, fearing what he might do if he were left at large, put him back into prison the moment Kamala's health showed a slight improvement. He had been free for just eleven days.

In June 1934, as much to take his mind off his wife's

deteriorating condition as anything, Jawaharlal Nehru began to write his autobiography, an elegant and fascinating portrait of his life and of his own mind. The 976-page manuscript was completed in nine months. When it was published in 1936, it bore the simple dedication "To Kamala, who is no more." The brave and long-suffering Mrs. Jawaharlal Nehru, barely older than the century, had succumbed to tuberculosis in a sanatorium in Lausanne on February 28, 1936. Despite (or perhaps because of) the long periods of neglect of the relationship, Jawaharlal was devastated. He had sent her to Europe the previous May in the hope that she would improve, but in September her doctors had cabled him that she was in critical condition, and the British suspended his sentence to enable him to be at her side. He joined her at a clinic in Badenweiler in Nazi Germany (where he made it a point to make his purchases from Jewish shopkeepers), then moved her to Lausanne, but it was all in vain.

Kamala's had been a deeply unhappy life, marked by a sense of social and intellectual inadequacy, afflicted by severe illness (her tuberculosis had been first diagnosed three years into her marriage, in 1919), punctuated by personal tragedy (the death of her infant son two days after his birth in 1925, a miscarriage in 1928), and undermined by her husband's overwhelming preoccupation with nationalist politics, which left him little time or inclination to be an attentive husband. Jawaharlal's prison diaries and correspondence in the 1920s hardly mention her, and even after they grew closer in the last few years of her life, it is clear their mental outlooks and personal values had little in common. But she was a loyal supporter of her husband's politics, and believed passionately in such issues as the education of girls and the ending of Hindu-Muslim conflict. The marriage was its best in the last half-dozen years of her life. Jawaharlal and Kamala rediscovered their intimacy on holiday in Ceylon in 1931, and their affection grew to such an extent that, toward the end of her life, even British Intelligence concluded that Jawaharlal was a "devoted husband." Jawaharlal ironically recalled seeing pictures of Kamala and himself being sold on the Indian sidewalks with the caption "Adarsh Jodi" ("Ideal Couple"). After her death Jawaharlal kept a photo of Kamala and a small urn of her ashes with him at all times, even in prison, and in his will he requested that her ashes be mingled with his own.

The book he dedicated to her, his *Autobiography*, was an astounding success in Britain and the West, and established Jawaharlal Nehru firmly in the world's imagination as the leader of modern India. Mahatma Gandhi, with his baffling fasts and prayers and penchant for enemas, stood for the spirit of an older tradition that imperialism could not suppress, but Jawaharlal's book spoke for the free India of the future. Though it was written entirely in a British prison, there is no rancor against the British, only against imperialism and exploitation. His rationality, his breadth of learning, his secular outlook, his moral indignation at the subjugation of his people, and the lucid fluency of his writing, attested to his own, and his country's, place in the world of the twentieth century that was still taking shape.

Of that place, Jawaharlal had no doubt, and the integrity of his convictions remained unwavering. On his way back by air from Switzerland with Kamala's ashes he was obliged to transit through the airport in Rome. Mussolini, Italy's Fascist dictator, sent a message of condolence and asked to meet with the Indian nationalist hero. A man of lesser principle might have seen this as an opportunity to win some international prominence for himself and his cause, but Jawaharlal, whose abhorrence of fascism was, if anything, even greater than his distaste of imperialism, firmly refused the invitation. At a time when many right-wing British politicians, a certain Winston Churchill included, had been, to say the least, ambivalent about the Fascist rulers of Germany, Italy, and Spain, Nehru's stubborn adherence to principle in the face of Italian persistence marked him as an uncommon figure of the age.

His stature had been diminished neither by imprisonment nor absence abroad; indeed, while he was in Europe the Congress elected him once more as its president for 1936. This was again Gandhi's doing; he saw Jawaharlal as a vital bridge to the radical left within the nationalist movement. In 1934, the Congress Socialist Party had been formed and the Mahatma had made clear his disagreement with its platform. Jawaharlal, whom the Socialists hoped would lead them in a revolt against Gandhi, had stayed within the establishment's fold, helping forestall an irrevocable split. Once again now, at Lucknow in April 1936, he delivered a presidential address that was strongly leftist in both tone and content, while presiding over a session whose resolutions were anything but. The Indian capitalist and benefactor of

Gandhi, G. D. Birla, wrote that Nehru's speech "was thrown into the waste paper basket. . . . Jawaharlalji seems to be like a typical English democrat who takes defeat in a sporting spirit. He seems to be [keen on] giving expression to his ideology, but he realizes that action is impossible and so does not press for it." Under Gandhi's influence, Jawaharlal even appointed a Working Committee for the party packed with moderates and conservatives.

Jawaharlal's personal finances were in poor shape for much of the 1930s; until supplemented by royalties from his best-selling autobiography, he could barely make ends meet after Motilal's death, having to maintain the large establishment at Anand Bhavan in Allahabad and support his extended family. He gave his sister Krishna (Betty) away during a brief spell out of jail in October 1933, but could not afford the traditional trousseau, let alone the "Nehru wedding camp" that Motilal had arranged for his own wedding in 1916. "You do not much look like a bride," Jawaharlal is said to have observed ruefully as he went to collect his sister for the ceremony. (Typically, he redressed matters by picking a red rose out of a vase and tucking it into her hair.) And yet he refused all offers of help, even when doing so might have eased the living conditions of his ailing wife. Birla, at whose home Mahatma Gandhi could often be found, discreetly offered Jawaharlal a monthly stipend to free his mind of financial worries. Jawaharlal turned it down, furious that any capitalist could presume to place him on his payroll.

The British had declared that elections would be held to form new provincial assemblies under the Government of India Act of 1935 (which was to come into effect on April Fool's Day 1937 as the new Constitution of British India). Jawaharlal wanted to settle for nothing short of full independence, but was outmaneuvered by his party elders into a collective decision to contest the elections. Indeed, as party president he had to lead the campaign, a task for which, with the adulation he excited among the masses, he was ideally suited. He roused the crowds as no one but the Mahatma could. He was initially less successful with his own party leaders, whose complaints against his style of functioning led the Mahatma to send him a confidential but severe rebuke for his "magisterial manner" and his arrogance to his senior colleagues:

> You are in office by their unanimous choice but you are not in power yet. To put you in office was an attempt to find you in power quicker than you would otherwise have been.

Thus reminded of whom he owed his position to, a chastened Jawaharlal mended his ways.

Electioneering brought out the best in Jawaharlal. He pounded tirelessly through the country on foot, by bicycle, in the back of a cart or the front of a car, by tonga, ekka, and even more exotic forms of locomotion (horseback, elephant, and camel), by canoe, paddleboat, steamship, train, and plane. By his own calculation he covered some 50,000 miles in 130 days of campaigning, with only 1,600 of these by air (his campaign plane was itself a first in India). The crowds turned out in their tens of thousands to greet him, and on one occasion they were packed so thick that he could only reach the rostrum by walking on their shoulders, which he did to general good cheer (though he realized only later that he should have taken off his shoes first). The reserved aristocrat came alive before a large audience; his speeches, whether in Hindi or English, were always clear, direct, easily understood if somewhat lecturing (the Communists' nickname for him was "the Professor"). His stamina was astonishing, accommodating innumerable engagements and several twenty-four-hour days. Somewhat remote and yet so palpably engaging, obviously well-bred yet capable of losing his temper in incandescent rages that passed as quickly as they came, handsome as no other Indian politician was, Jawaharlal Nehru at forty-six was the glamorous face of Indian nationalism just as Gandhi was its otherworldly deity. About him there was a presence that went beyond mere charisma; people who could understand neither English nor Hindi came just to catch a glimpse of him, and a British official reported in surprisingly generous terms to his superiors that "there is no doubt that his manliness, frankness and reputation for sacrifice attracts a large public." His reelection to a second consecutive presidential term for 1937 (after the conservative Sardar Vallabhbhai Patel withdrew his challenge) underscored the extent to which he had outstripped his rivals within the party. The Nobel Prize-winning poet Rabindranath Tagore hailed Jawaharlal as the embodiment of spring itself, "representing the season of youth and triumphant joy."

The campaign marked his rediscovery of India and of the Indian masses — till then, he said, "I had not fully realized what they were and what they meant to India" — and confirmed him as Gandhi's most likely successor at the head of the Congress Party. Yet Jawaharlal was always conscious of the risk that power, and in particular mass adulation, could turn one's head. Within a year of the election this unusual democrat pseudonymously authored a remarkable attack upon himself in the *Modern Review:*

> [Nehru] has all the makings of a dictator in him — vast popularity, a strong will directed to a well-defined purpose, energy, pride, organizational capacity, ability, hardness, and, with all his love of the crowd, an intolerance of others and a certain contempt of the weak and the inefficient. . . . From the far north to Cape Comorin he has gone like some triumphant Caesar, leaving a trail of glory and legend behind him. . . . [I]s it his will to power that is driving him from crowd to crowd? His conceit is already formidable. He must be checked. We want no Caesars.

The election campaign inevitably crystallized the implicit choice Jawaharlal had consistently made each time he was confronted with it — nationalism above socialism. His first campaign speech in Bombay, an assault on capitalism, won him cheers from the sans-culottes and such opprobrium from businessmen that the British thought his leadership would divide the party irrevocably and lead it to electoral disaster. Once again, they were proved wrong; but this was at least partly because

Jawaharlal chose not to go so far as to damage the party. The Congress election manifesto made no mention of socialism. What it did focus on was the constitutional system built into the Government of India Act, in particular the pernicious Communal Award, under which the British had again sought to divide Indians by creating seventeen separate electorates for different communities. The principal purpose of seeking election, the Congress declared, was to undo this British perfidy by wrecking the constitutional system from within and demanding full freedom and unfettered democracy rather than political half-measures.

The allocation of seats under the Act was deliberately stacked against the Congress, in particular by arrangements giving the Muslims and other minorities (and therefore the parties seeking to represent such narrower identities) a larger number of seats than their proportion of the population would have warranted; and the rural poor, Gandhi's natural base (and to a great extent Jawaharlal's), were denied the vote altogether. Yet the election results exceeded the expectations of even the most optimistic Congressman. The Congress Party contested 1,161 of the 1,585 seats at stake; it won 716, an astonishing 62 percent of the seats contested. This was despite restrictions on the franchise, which gave disproportionate influence to the educated and the well-off by granting the vote to only 36 million out of India's 300 million population, and the active hostility of the governmental machinery. Further, the Congress emerged as the largest single party in nine of the eleven provinces; in six of them it had an outright majority. Jawaharlal interpreted this as a mandate to reject the Government of India Act and demand a Constituent Assembly instead, but his partymen preferred immediate office to future freedom — jam today rather than bread tomorrow. They accepted his draft resolution describing the election results as a repudiation of the Act, but added a clause (dictated by Gandhi) authorizing Congressmen to take office in each province if they were satisfied that they could rule without interference by the British-appointed governor. Once again Jawaharlal came close to resigning. Once again, he chose to put party unity ahead of his own convictions. ("Just as the King can do no wrong," he said after having been outvoted by his colleagues, "the Working Committee can do no wrong.") In July 1937, Congress ministries were formed in six provinces.

Meanwhile, the Muslim League had awoken from a long slumber. After years of inactivity crowned by political success (since the British government tended to grant the League's princely leaders everything they asked for, and in the Communal Award actually exceeded the League's own requests) the party's grandees began to take note with concern of the mass mobilization led by the Congress. In response, they invited Jinnah back from his long self-exile in London and made him "permanent president" of the League in April 1936.

The British government was not averse to this development. As early as 1888, the Congress's founder, Allan Octavian Hume, felt obliged to denounce British attempts to promote Hindu-Muslim division by fostering "the devil's . . . dismal doctrine of discord and disunion." The strategy was hardly surprising for an imperial power.

"*Divide et impera* was the old Roman motto," wrote Lord Elphinstone after the 1857 Mutiny, "and it should be ours." Promoting communal discord became conscious British policy. In December 1887 — at a time when the Congress's first Muslim president, Badruddin Tyabji, was striving to unite Hindus and Muslims in a common cause — the pro-British judge and Muslim educationist Sir Syed Ahmed Khan was arguing in a speech in Lucknow that the departure of the British would inevitably lead to civil war. The numerical advantage of Hindus over Muslims, he argued, would give them unfair advantage in a democratic India; imperial rule by the Christian British, fellow "people of the book," was therefore preferable. In 1906, a deputation of Muslim notables led by the Aga Khan and seeking separate privileges for Muslims was received by the British viceroy, and the Muslim League was born.

But in its thirty years of existence, the League had failed to become a potent force in national politics. Jinnah formulated an effective strategy to raise the League to political prominence as the "third party" in a struggle involving the British and the Congress. He argued that he too was an Indian nationalist who sought greater rights from the British, but he aimed to achieve these by constitutional means, while protecting the interests of the Muslim community. In his public speeches he portrayed the Congress as a Hindu-dominated party whose triumph would threaten the religious identity of Indian Muslims and displace their preferred language, Urdu. More privately, he was not averse to suggesting to the League's affluent patrons that Jawaharlal Nehru's dangerous socialism was a threat to the economic interests of the Muslim landed and commercial elites. Nehru bridled at what he saw as Jinnah's pretensions, challenging the representativeness of the League's leadership: "I come into greater touch with the Muslim masses," he declared acidly, "than most of the members of the Muslim League." Asserting the Congress's claim to speak for all Indians of whatever faith, he rejected the notion that the League (a "drawing-room party") had any valid place: "There are only two forces in the country, the Congress and the Government. Those who are standing midway shall have to choose between the two."

Jawaharlal's contempt was based both on his distaste for communal bigotry (he often condemned the Hindu Mahasabha, the principal political vehicle of Hindu chauvinism, in the same breath) and his political judgment. The latter was borne out by the 1937 election results. Under the British provisions for separate communal electorates, 7,319,445 votes were cast by Muslim voters for Muslim candidates; only 4.4 percent of these, 321,772, went to the Muslim League. In other words, the League had been overwhelmingly repudiated by the very community in whose name it claimed to speak. Instead Muslim voters had voted for a wide variety of other parties, from the landholding Unionists in the Punjab to a peasants and tenants' party in Bengal, and even for the Congress, which foolishly had run very few Muslim candidates (it put up 58 candidates in the 482 seats reserved for Muslims and won 26 of those races). Victorious Muslim politicians were more interested in securing power in their provinces than in supporting Jinnah's advocacy of a pan-Indian Muslim identity.

In mid-1937, therefore, the League was not a serious

threat to Congress ascendancy. Defeated in his wish to keep his party out of British-supervised ministerial office (under a Constitution that did not even grant Dominion status, let alone independence), Jawaharlal stayed president of the Congress but went into the political equivalent of a sulk. He was in fact away on a tour of Burma and Malaya when the decision to accept office was taken by his colleagues. He refused to serve on the Congress Parliamentary Board which was set up to give party guidance to the provincial ministries. Yet he became caught up in one of the most controversial episodes of his political career — the failure of the Congress to accept the offer of the Muslim League to form a coalition government in Jawaharlal's own province, U.P.

The League had won twenty-seven of the sixty-four Muslim seats in the U.P. legislature; the Congress, which had only run nine Muslim candidates, had won none, but it had enjoyed overwhelming success in the "general" seats (those not reserved for any particular community) and, with a majority in the legislature as a whole, was in a position to form a ministry on its own. As party president, Nehru initiated a "mass contact" program for Congress workers with the Muslim population, in order to bring more of them into the nationalist movement. The League saw this as a threat; its political success depended on its being able to credibly claim that it was the sole spokesman for India's Muslims. The two visions were clearly incompatible, yet the League began negotiating with the Congress to form a joint government in which the League would nominate two Muslim ministers. The lead Congress negotiator was a Muslim, Maulana Azad; the lead League negotiator was Chaudhuri Khaliquzzaman, formerly a close friend of Jawaharlal's who had often enjoyed his hospitality, staying at Anand Bhavan whenever he visited Allahabad. The two negotiators came close to an agreement. The League was even willing to merge its identity in the provincial legislature with that of the Congress, but the deal finally foundered on the League's insistence that its legislators would be free to vote differently on "communal issues."

This could never be acceptable to Nehru. Jawaharlal saw the communal card as rank political opportunism. In a passionate letter to his old friend Khaliquzzaman, he asked: "Why should I accept it [the League] as the representatives of the Muslims of India when I know it represents [only] the handful of Muslims at the top who deliberately seek refuge in the name of religion to avoid discussing mass problems?" The Congress of Jawaharlal Nehru was committed to land reform; the League was in thrall to big Muslim landowners. Jawaharlal was also conscious that, as his Muslim colleague Abdul Walli wrote to him, "once the Congress enters into a pact with the Muslim League it loses the right to ask the Muslims to join it." Jawaharlal believed at the very core of his being that the nationalist movement had to be a movement of the masses, animated by political and economic considerations, not religious ones. In his *Autobiography*, he had already written of being "troubled . . . at the growth of this religious element in our politics, both on the Hindu and Muslim side":

> I did not like it at all. Much that Moulvies and Maulanas and Swamis and the like said in their public addresses seemed to me unfortunate. Their

> history and sociology and economics appeared to me all wrong, and the religious twist that was given to everything prevented all clear thinking. Even some of Gandhiji's phrases sometimes jarred upon me — thus his frequent reference to Ram Raj as a golden age which was to return.

It is telling that Jawaharlal denounced the use of religious imagery in politics quite impartially, even reproaching the Mahatma for evoking Hindu mythology in painting a vision of post-British India. To Jinnah's communal politics Jawaharlal opposed his secular and rationalist beliefs; there would be no question of allowing the Congress to become the party of any one community. From such a perspective, giving the Muslim League the respectability of holding ministerial office in U.P. as the representative of the province's Muslims stuck in Jawaharlal's craw.

Some — most notably Maulana Azad himself, in his posthumous memoir — have suggested that Jawaharlal's implacable opposition scuttled a possible deal and set the seal on the widening divergence between the parties that would ultimately culminate in the partition of India. There is no doubt that Jawaharlal was not in favor of a deal with the Muslim League, but the negotiations appear to have collapsed because of the intractability of the conditions posed by both sides, rather than solely because of his opposition to them. In any case, other political developments at the time do not suggest that this episode deserves to be given quite so much weight in the history of the freedom struggle. Strikingly, a Muslim

League legislator in U.P., Hafiz Ibrahim, resigned from his party and ran again for his own seat as a Congress candidate. Despite virulent opposition from the League, Ibrahim was elected, giving the Congress an elected "Muslim" seat in the provincial assembly. The Congress also formed the government in the overwhelmingly Muslim North-West Frontier Province, where the "Frontier Gandhi," Khan Abdul Ghaffar Khan, had led his red-shirted nonviolent Khudai Khidmatgars ("Servants of God") into the party. At that stage Jawaharlal's (and the Congress's) claim to speak for Indians of all communities, and his refusal to concede the Muslims of India to the League, remained entirely tenable.

In July 1937 Jinnah issued a statement deploring the Congress's "mass contact" policy with Muslims: "There is plenty of scope for Pandit Jawaharlal Nehru to improve his own people, the Hindus," he declared. Nehru replied immediately: "Not being religiously or communally inclined, I venture to think of my people as the Indian people as a whole." Two months earlier he had confessed to the press: "Personally I find it difficult to think of any question on communal lines. I think on political and economic lines." In those fundamentally irreconcilable attitudes lay the seeds of a divide that would, over the next decade, tear the country apart.

6

"In the Name of God, Go!": 1937–1945

To the surprise of both their supporters and their critics, the Congress ministries in the provinces conducted themselves as able stewards of the governmental system of the British Raj. For the most part they did little to dismantle oppressive British laws, and in some cases proved as zealous in arresting radicals as the British themselves had been. The delighted governor of Madras, Lord Erskine, commented privately that his Congress chief minister, the conservative C. Rajagopalachari, was "even too much of a Tory for me." In the exuberance of their first crack at governance, some Congress ministries failed to pay sufficient heed to Muslim sensibilities in their appointments, regulations, or promotion of nationalist (often Hindu) symbols. Jawaharlal observed all this with dismay; having already objected to his party's assumption of office, he was distressed by his colleagues' willingness to serve the colonial system in a manner that was antithetical to the Congress's declared policies and principles. Yet, typically, he put party loyalty above private conviction ("we cannot agitate against ourselves") and spoke in defense of the Congress ministries in public, leading his radical supporters to write him off as a "parlor socialist" incapable of leading genuine revolutionary change. His presidency ended in the proverbial whimper, with his rival Subhas Chandra Bose's election to office for 1938.

Increasingly disenchanted with the compromises he saw his party making domestically, Jawaharlal — pausing only to establish a pro-Congress newspaper in Lucknow, the *National Herald* — turned his attention to world affairs, in particular the civil wars then raging in Spain and China, as well as the Italian invasion of Abyssinia. He organized demonstrations against Mussolini, a boycott of Japanese goods (over that country's conduct in China), a China relief fund, and a medical unit to serve there. When his mother passed away, after a long illness, in January 1938, and since his daughter, Indira, was studying at Oxford, Jawaharlal decided to travel to Europe. This time there were no government-imposed restrictions on his activities, and he pursued an openly political agenda, meeting with Egyptian nationalists in Alexandria before traveling overland to Spain as a guest of the Republican government. He spent five days in Barcelona, braving Franco's air raids, and felt strongly tempted to join the

International Brigades battling fascism there.[6] He tried to arrange for the settlement of European Jewish refugees in India, despite stringent conditions imposed by the British authorities. In England, buoyed by the increased stature that had followed the success of his *Autobiography*, he addressed public meetings at Trafalgar Square and at the Royal Albert Hall, lunched with editors, journalists, and members of Parliament, and even met the new viceroy, Lord Linlithgow, who had succeeded Willingdon in 1936 and was then on holiday in Britain. At this meeting he declared to the nonplussed viceroy that he "gave England at the outside ten years before India [became] independent."

The same spirit revealed itself in a fiery address to an international conference in Paris on the bombing of civilians, followed by two days in Munich (where he refused to meet with Nazi officials despite the German government's entreaties) and an emotional visit to Czechoslovakia on the verge of its surrender to German might and Anglo-French complicity. Nehru was in Geneva when the League of Nations met to discuss the Czech crisis, then in London again at the height of the appeasement drama (where amid the general panic he

[6] He spent an afternoon with the American and British battalions of the International Brigades and wrote of the deep sense of longing he felt to join them: "something in me wanted to stay on this inhospitable looking hillside which sheltered so much human courage, so much of what was worthwhile in life." But he was nearly fifty years old, and he knew he had a greater cause to serve in his own country.

was outfitted with a gas mask). His views were clear and uncompromising; he was hostile both to British imperialism and to European fascism, and he would place India firmly on the side of democracy in the inevitable conflict, provided the British proved their democratic credentials by granting freedom to India first. Sickened by Chamberlain's sellout at Munich and unable to obtain a Russian visa for a planned overland return home through Central Asia, Jawaharlal arrived home at the end of 1938, ready again for domestic politics.

The situation at home was hardly more encouraging than the dire circumstances abroad. Jinnah had proved a skilled leader of the League, making up for its defeat in the Muslim-majority provinces of Punjab and Bengal by in effect co-opting the victorious leaders there onto the League platform. The Congress itself was riven by infighting. Its acceptance of office had both alienated its left wing and made it vulnerable to wholly specious charges of imposing "Hindu majority rule" on the Muslim minority. Subhas Bose had not proved a successful leader as president; more to the point, he fell out with Mahatma Gandhi. When Bose ran for reelection in early 1939, Gandhi openly encouraged a more conservative candidate to challenge him. Bose's subsequent victory was seen by the Mahatma himself as Gandhi's defeat. But the ambitious and hotheaded Bose went further, trying to force the old guard out and assert his dominance over the party. The Mahatma, who was as shrewd as he was saintly, orchestrated a revolt against Bose in the Working Committee that forced Bose's resignation from the presidency.

Jawaharlal had little patience for Bose and his ways, but could not bring himself to approve of the defenestration of the party's elected president. As a result he came across as ambivalent on the divisions within the party, with Bose in particular accusing him of betrayal and of siding with the conservatives. Jawaharlal's sympathies were hardly with the Congress's right wing, but he was swayed by his admiration for Gandhi and his distaste for what he saw as Bose's dangerous flirtations with fascism and his political inconsistencies. Nor did he appreciate Bose's provoking the party into a split when the international situation called for unity at home. So, though he did not join the organized revolt against Bose, he separately resigned from Bose's Working Committee. Some cynics saw him as merely seeking to emerge on the winning side; and his rupture with Bose over the episode was to be permanent. ("Quite a remarkable feat," Jawaharlal mused, "to displease almost everybody concerned.")

As war clouds gathered over Europe in 1939, Jawaharlal Nehru's focus at home was on two domestic issues: the battle for civil liberties in the "princely states" (ruled nominally by maharajahs and nawabs under British tutelage, but therefore out of the reach of normal Indian politics) and the task of long-term national economic planning. He served as president of the All-India States People's Conference and as chairman of the National Planning Committee set up by ministers of industry of the Congress-ruled provinces. In both cases his contributions were vital: he hammered the first nails into the coffin of monarchical rule in India (whose collapse was made inevitable by Nehru's efforts to organize resistance in what was called the "States' Congress") and the first pegs into the wall on which the trappings of Indian socialism would eventually be hung.

Meanwhile, the shadow of what would be known as the Second World War was looming. As early as 1927, in moving a resolution on the international situation at the Madras Congress, Jawaharlal had foreseen the prospect of another major war in Europe. His view was that India should stay out of any such conflict until she had obtained her freedom from the imperialists who would seek to exploit her. But his abhorrence of fascism was so great that he would gladly lead a free India into war on the side of the democracies, provided that choice was made by Indians and not imposed upon them by the British. When Germany's invasion of Poland on September 1, 1939 led Britain to declare war upon it, Indians noted the irony of the English fighting to defend the sovereignty of a weak country resisting the brute force of foreign conquest — precisely what Indian nationalists were doing against British imperialism. So Britain would fight Germany for doing to Poland what Britain had been doing to India for nearly two hundred years. Yet it would have found allies in the anti-Fascist Congress governments in the provinces and among Congress legislators in the Central Assembly. Gandhi and Rajagopalachari were effusive in their immediate professions of support to Britain in her hour of peril. Lord Linlithgow, however, did not so much as make a pretense of consulting India's elected leaders before declaring war on Germany on behalf of India.

Jawaharlal Nehru was in China when war broke out.

He was enormously attracted to the idea of India enjoying close relations with another great ancient Asian civilization, and he entertained romantic notions of a grand eastern alliance between the two as they each emerged from the incubus of colonialism and rose to the challenge of developing their fractured societies. He got along well with Chiang Kai-shek but had also arranged to visit the communist revolutionary Mao Tse-tung when news of the war obliged him to cut short his trip and return home. The news left him seething. He blamed British appeasement for the fall of Spain to the Fascists, the betrayal of Ethiopia to the Italians, and the selling out of Czechoslovakia to the Nazis: he wanted India to have no part of the responsibility for British policy, which he saw as designed to protect the narrow class interests of a few imperialists. Why, he asked, should Indians be expected to make sacrifices to preserve British rule over them? How could a subject India be ordered to fight for a free Poland? A free and democratic India, on the other hand, would gladly fight for freedom and democracy.

Under his direction, the Congress Working Committee adopted a resolution making this case (while rejecting Bose's demand that civil disobedience be launched immediately). Nehru made no secret of his own anti-Nazi views; his dislike of fascism ran so deep that he dismissed a sub-editor at the *National Herald* who, in an excess of patriotism, had published a pro-German headline. All he wanted was some indication from the British government of respect for his position so that India and Britain could then gladly "join in a struggle for freedom." The Congress leaders made it clear to the viceroy that all they needed was a declaration that India would be given the chance to determine its own future after the war. The Congress position was greeted with understanding and even some approval in left-wing circles in Britain, and Labour Party politicians, including Clement Attlee (a former member of the Simon Commission and a future prime minister) pressed the government to come to terms with Indian aspirations. But Linlithgow, who had already revealed his lack of tact in making the declaration of war, now revealed his lack of imagination as well. Jawaharlal tried his best to appeal privately to the viceroy in remarkably conciliatory terms, but found him "heavy of body and slow of mind, solid as a rock and with almost a rock's lack of awareness." Linlithgow failed to respond to the Congress's implicit call for talks on the issue and instead turned to the Muslim League for support.

The Congress had in fact hoped for a joint approach on the war issue with the League. Jinnah was invited to the Congress Working Committee meeting in September, but refused to attend. Jawaharlal nonetheless met with him, the second time together with Gandhi, and a convergence of views seemed to be emerging. The viceroy's statement in October 1939 emphatically rejecting the Congress position, however, prompted the Working Committee, with Jawaharlal in the lead, to order all its provincial ministries to resign rather than continue to serve a war effort in which they had been denied an honorable role. The decision was taken on a point of principle, but politically it proved a monumental blunder. It deprived the Congress of their only leverage with the British government, cast aside the fruits of their electoral success, and presented Jinnah with a golden opportunity. He broke off talks with the Congress — declaring the day of the Congress resignations a "day of deliverance" — and turned to the viceroy instead.

Two years in the political wilderness after the electoral setbacks of 1937 had already transformed the League. Congress rule in many provinces had unwittingly increased Muslim concern, even alarm, about the implications of democratic majoritarian rule in a country so overwhelmingly Hindu. Many Muslims began to see themselves as a political and economic minority, and the League spoke to their insecurities. Jinnah had begun to come to the conclusion that the only effective answer to the Congress's political strength would be separation — the partition of the country to create an independent state in the Muslim-majority areas of the northwest and east. This demand would be enshrined in the League's Lahore resolution of March 23, 1940 calling for the creation of Pakistan. Jawaharlal and his fellow Congress leaders were largely oblivious of the change of thinking among many League members, manifest in an increasingly populist political strategy (it was only in 1939, for instance, that Jinnah began to learn Urdu and to don the *achkan* for official photographs, actions reminiscent of that old saw from the French Revolution: "I am their leader — I must follow them").

In October 1939 Jinnah persuaded Linlithgow to enlist the League as an interlocutor equal to the Congress and as the sole representative of India's Muslims, a position to which its electoral results did not yet entitle it. The viceroy, anxious to prevent Congress-League unity on the war issue, consented. The League's policy, he observed, was now the most important obstacle to any talk of Indian independence, and therefore needed to be encouraged. That November Jinnah was invited, for the first time, to broadcast a special message to Muslims on the occasion of the Id festival — an explicit recognition of the League president as the spokesman of the Muslim community. Nehru and the Congress simply saw such claims as illegitimate and premised on bigotry; they did not do enough to address the real crisis of confidence brewing in the Muslim community at the prospect of majority rule.

That was the month Jawaharlal marked his fiftieth birthday. It was a muted celebration, and the poet Sarojini Naidu captured the mood well in her birthday greetings: "I do not think that personal happiness, comfort, leisure, wealth . . . can have much place in your life. . . . Sorrow, suffering, anguish, strife, yes, these are the predestined gifts of life for you. . . . You are a man of destiny born to be alone in the midst of crowds — deeply loved, but little understood." It was an assessment that many, not least Jawaharlal's daughter, Indira, shared.

Through much of 1940 the Congress played a waiting game, hoping for British concessions. It was a period of a "phony stalemate" in India to match the "phony war" in Europe. Jawaharlal spent much of his time writing brilliant articles for the *National Herald*, none more moving than his paean, upon the fall of Paris, to "the France of the Revolution, the breaker of the Bastille and of all the bonds that hold the human body and spirit captive." Despite the provincial resignations, Gandhi was not in favor of outright civil disobedience. Jawaharlal, disillusioned by the Soviet Union's opportunistic conduct in the war, turned increasingly in his writings to the United States as a beacon of freedom and democracy. Together they compromised on what was called "partial noncooperation" with the British. The party was to prepare for satyagraha and nonviolent resistance, but to undertake no action that would undermine the British war effort. Gandhi and Jawaharlal had no desire to be seen as taking advantage of Britain's hour of peril.

Some of their colleagues were prepared to go even further and extend direct support to the war effort if there was a national government established in India to support it. But Linlithgow's thinking was far removed from even the most basic of Indian aspirations. (He wrote to London in April 1940: "I am not too keen to start talking about a period after which British rule will have ceased in India. I suspect that that day is very remote and I feel the [less] we say about it in all probability the better.") When the official response of the government came in August 1940, it was a derisory offer to associate a few "representative Indians" with the viceroy's toothless advisory councils. Jawaharlal rejected this utterly. Civil disobedience seemed the only answer.

The government decided not to wait for what Jawaharlal might do. They arrested him on October 30, 1940 and, after a trial distinguished by a magnificent statement by the accused ("it is the British Empire itself that is on trial before the bar of the world"), sentenced him to four years in prison. The conditions of his detention were unusually harsh, with a number of petty indignities inflicted upon him, in particular relating to his ability to send or receive mail, which deprived him of the solace that letters had provided over the years. Cleaning, washing, and gardening became his principal chores in prison. He was soon joined in jail by his brother-in-law Ranjit Pandit, Nan's husband, who had a greener thumb, and their jail garden flourished. There was time for reading and reflection; once again Jawaharlal's thoughts turned to the historical forces that had shaped his country, and he began writing, with his now customary rapidity, what was to become a monumental work of Indian nationalism, *The Discovery of India*.

In December 1941, despite the opposition of Winston Churchill, the War Cabinet in London authorized the release of all the imprisoned Congressmen. Jawaharlal hoped in vain for some policy declaration by the British that would enable him to commit India to the Allied cause, but the reactionary Churchill and his blinkered representatives in New Delhi went the other way, with Churchill (whose subsequent beatification as an apostle of freedom seems all the more preposterous) explicitly declaring that the principles of the Atlantic Charter would not apply to India. The "Tory" Congressman Rajagopalachari even persuaded the Working Committee to offer Britain the defense cooperation of a free India, but the British did not take the bait. This was all the more inexplicable in the face of the rout of British forces in Asia: Singapore fell in February, Burma in March; the Japanese were at India's gates in the east, and Subhas Bose, who had fled British India, fashioned an "Indian National Army" in mid-1941 out of prisoners of war to fight alongside the Japanese. Jawaharlal had no desire to see one emperor's rule supplanted by another's: he started organizing the Congress to prepare for resistance to the Japanese. Chiang Kai-shek visited India to counsel support for the British, then urged U.S. president Roosevelt to persuade the British to change their policies. American sympathy was matched by that of the Labour Party in the War Cabinet. Clement Attlee persuaded his colleagues to send the socialist Sir Stafford Cripps to India in early 1942 with an offer of Dominion status after the war, with the possibility of partition.

Cripps was already a legend in British politics, a former solicitor-general who had been expelled from the Labour Party in 1939 for advocating a united front with the Conservatives (which of course came to pass during the war), and who combined an ascetic vegetarianism with a flamboyant ego ("there, but for the grace of God, goes God," Churchill remarked of him). Cripps had visited India after the outbreak of war in 1939 and knew many Indian leaders; he considered Jawaharlal a friend. Yet the Cripps mission was welcomed by Jinnah, but foundered on the opposition of the Congress. Gandhi objected principally because the British proposal appeared to concede the idea of partition; he memorably called the offer "a post-dated cheque" (an imaginative journalist added, "on a crashing bank") and urged its rejection. Rajagopalachari was willing to accept the proposal. Congress president Maulana Azad insisted that the defense of India should be the responsibility of Indian representatives, not the unelected government of India led by the British viceroy, and it was on this issue that Jawaharlal refused to compromise. Cripps was inclined to give in, and spoke of an Indian national government running the country's defense with the viceroy functioning as a figurehead (like the British king). But he had exceeded his instructions: the egregious Churchill ("I hate Indians. They are a beastly people with a beastly religion"), abetted by the reluctance of the hidebound viceroy, Linlithgow, and the diplomatic ineptitude of the commander in chief, Lord Wavell, scuttled the negotiations. Now obliged to disown his own gloss on the offer, Cripps, to his discredit, publicly blamed the Indians and in particular Gandhi for his failure — a misrepresentation of the discussions for which Jawaharlal never forgave him.

Nonetheless, Jawaharlal remained an outspoken advocate of the Allied cause, even threatening guerrilla warfare against the Japanese if they were to invade — an issue on which he earned a sharp rebuke from the Mahatma. His attempts to enlist American sympathy for the Indian case in the negotiations with the British, however, did not succeed; Roosevelt, who might have been able to temper the racist imperialism of Churchill, declined to intervene. Gandhi, increasingly exasperated by the British, argued that Jawaharlal's pro-Allied position had won India no concessions. His public message to the Government was to "leave India to God or anarchy." Jawaharlal, ever the Harrovian Anglophile, quoted Cromwell (in a conscious echo of the Harrovian Amery, who had used the same words just two years earlier in Parliament in calling for Neville Chamberlain's resignation as prime minister): "You have sat too long here for any good you have been doing. Depart, I say, and let us have done with you. In the name of God, go!" On August 7, 1942 in Bombay, the All-India Congress Committee, at the Mahatma's urging, adopted a resolution moved by Nehru, and seconded by Patel, calling upon Britain to — in a journalistic paraphrase that became more famous than the actual words of the resolution — "Quit India." (Gandhi's own preferred phrase was "Do or Die.") Within thirty-six hours the Congress leaders were under arrest. Mahatma Gandhi was incarcerated in the Aga Khan's palace in Poona; Jawaharlal Nehru and the rest in Ahmadnagar Fort.

Jawaharlal was always a curious combination of the idealist intellectual and the man of action. On the way to jail, an incident occurred that brought out the latter quality. At the station in Poona, when the train made an unscheduled stop, a crowd of people recognized Jawaharlal and ran toward his compartment. The police tried to prevent them approaching him by resorting to a *lathi*-charge. Outraged at seeing unarmed civilians being beaten by police staves, Jawaharlal leapt out onto the platform through the narrow window of the train to remonstrate with the police. Though he was fifty-three, it took four policemen to restrain him and force him back onto the train — and the officer in charge apologized personally for the incident.

Some of that fury communicated itself to the populace at large. For all of the Mahatma's devotion to nonviolence, his jailing, together with the rest of the Congress leadership, left the Quit India movement in the hands of the young and the hotheaded. An underground movement was born, which actively resorted to acts of sabotage. Ordinary people took improbable risks to hoist the national flag on government buildings. Young newsboys added sotto voce subversion to their sales cries: "*Times of India.* Quit India. *Times of India.* Quit India." In the weeks after the arrests, no day passed without reports of clashes between demonstrators and police. The British responded with ruthless repression, firing upon unarmed protestors, killing dozens every week, flogging offenders, and censoring (and closing down) nationalist newspapers. "Quit India" became the drumbeat of a national awakening, but all it did was to prolong the nation's continued subjugation.

In this climate, there was to be no respite for Jawaharlal; this became his longest spell in prison, a total of 1,040 days, or more than 34 months, from August 9, 1942 to June 15, 1945. Initially cut off from all communication (even newspapers), the Congress leaders were gradually allowed a few limited privileges, but Jawaharlal rejected many of the humiliating conditions imposed upon him. "I do not fancy being treated like a wild beast in a cage with occasional rope allowed so that I can move a few feet if I behave myself," he wrote to his sister Nan, imprisoned elsewhere. ". . . Where force prevents me from acting as I wish, I have to accept it, but I prefer to retain such freedom of mind and action as I possess." His freedom was not much: Jawaharlal's prison diary abounds in trivia, featuring the acquisition of new canvas shoes and the death of a cat inadvertently hit on the head by a cook. He read Proust, and learned Urdu poetry from Maulana Azad, for whom his friendship and respect deepened.

Nonetheless the prison experience was not without significance. Tempers frayed among the Congressmen;

the strain of prolonged incarceration proved unbearable for many, and Jawaharlal's close friend for thirty-five years, Syed Mahmud, obtained his release in 1944 by disowning the Congress resolution. Gandhi nearly died after a fast in 1943. And Jawaharlal finished *The Discovery of India*, which he had begun during his earlier stint in jail. Instead of the Marxian obsession with social and economic forces that characterized *Glimpses of World History*, Jawaharlal revealed an abiding fascination with the making of the Indian nation, its cultural and historical antecedents, and the continuity of the Indian heritage from the days of the Indus Valley Civilization to the privations of British rule. For all the weaknesses of the book — born from the circumstances of its composition, the lack of source material, and the absence of a skilled editor — it is a striking articulation of a view of Indian nationhood that transcended the petty pride of most nationalisms. To Nehru, India was a palimpsest on which many had written their contributions and none were to be disowned; the greatness of India lay in her diversity, the richness of her varied civilization, her willingness to absorb and accommodate disparate religions and ethnicities. It is a stirring evocation of the past as an instrument to explain the present and give hope for the future, and as such it is the primordial text in what was, ultimately, Jawaharlal Nehru's invention of India.

But before "Quit India" and prison consumed him, a major development had occurred on the personal front. In March 1942, his daughter, Indira, now twenty-four, married the man who had been courting her for nearly seven years, her mother's faithful admirer Feroze Gandhi.

If Kamala's impact on Jawaharlal's thought or action

is difficult to discern, she was indirectly responsible for the turn her daughter's life had taken. During her brief stint, between bouts of ill-health, as a Congress volunteer, Kamala went to address a college in Lucknow and fainted from the heat and exhaustion. The young student who rushed to her succor became a lifelong fan and soon followed her into active work for the Congress Party. His name was Feroze Gandhi.

Nehru's sister Betty described Feroze as enamored of Kamala "in a romantic, Dante-and-Beatrice way, content if he could just be near her." He dropped out of college to be at her side, and was in Lausanne at Kamala's deathbed. His fidelity to her mother was certainly a crucial factor in Indira's own attraction to the fair-skinned, stocky Parsi (a member of India's tiny Zoroastrian minority, descended from Persian refugees who had fled Muslim persecution in the seventh century, and no relation of the Mahatma). In India the development of such a relationship would have had severe obstacles to overcome, but Feroze and Indira both decided to study in England and became intimate there, Indira finally accepting Feroze's proposal of marriage on the steps of the Sacré-Coeur in Paris. When they returned to India they found the Nehru family, particularly Jawaharlal's sisters, implacably opposed to their marriage plans (an impecunious Parsi without a college degree for the only heir of the future leader of free India? The prospect, Nan averred, was out of the question). But Jawaharlal could not bring himself to stand in the way of the happiness of his only child. Though he tried to delay her decision, and though hate mail arriving at his residence left him in no doubt of the views of the self-appointed guardians of Hindu purity, Jawaharlal acquiesced in her wishes. He issued a statement to the press in February 1942. Marriage, he declared, was a personal affair; "on whomsoever my daughter's choice would have fallen, I would have accepted it or been false to the principles I have held." But he was careful enough to cite the Mahatma's blessing of the match, and to conduct the wedding according to Vedic Hindu rites.

Nehru often called his daughter "Indu-boy," a term of affection that could not but have reminded her of her duty to compensate for his lack of a son. His own relationship with his father had been paramount, and he tried to replicate it with Indira, particularly in their correspondence; but here she could not hold her own quite as he had been able to do. Jawaharlal was also far more of an absentee father than Motilal had been; there was no equivalent in his parental career of Motilal's risking all to intercede for him in Nabha, or of Motilal's sacrifice of wealth and security to advance the convictions (and ambitions) of his son. Where Jawaharlal had been the repository of all of Motilal's hopes for his country and his heritage, Indira was merely his daughter, and even the nickname "Indu-boy" seemed to suggest that was not somehow quite good enough.

Jawaharlal was in prison when Indira made him a grandfather, with the birth of Rajiv (a name chosen by Jawaharlal, since it means the same as "Kamala" — "lotus") on August 20, 1944. Indira paid him the quiet tribute of adding a middle name for her son that was a synonym of her father's name — "Ratna," which like

"Jawahar" means "jewel." That was the only good news in a period of torment for the Nehru family, all of whom were in jail in appalling conditions. Indira herself was out of prison only because she had been released on grounds of ill-health; she had contracted pleurisy, the same affliction that had laid Nan's husband, Ranjit Pandit, low, and which took his life in early 1944. Betty's husband, Raja Hutheesingh, also left jail beset by ailments from which he would never quite recover.

Personal setbacks were mirrored by political ones. With the Congress leadership in jail, the British moved to strengthen the position of Jinnah and the Muslim League, pressuring Jinnah's critics within the party to remain in the League and under his leadership. Muslim opponents of the Pakistan idea were dissuaded, sidelined, or (like Sir Sikandar Hyat Khan in Punjab and Allah Bux in Sind) died. The League formed governments (often with the votes of British members, and with Congress legislators in jail) in provinces where it had been routed in the elections, and enjoyed patronage appointments where formal office was not possible. The futility of the Quit India movement, which accomplished little but the Congress's own exclusion from national affairs, compounded the original blunder of the Congress in resigning its ministries. It had left the field free for the Muslim League, which emerged from the war immeasurably enhanced in power and prestige. Even the Mahatma, after his release from prison on health grounds in May 1944, held talks with Jinnah that seemed to confirm the latter's stature as an alternative center of power in the country.

On June 15, 1945, Jawaharlal and his Congress colleagues emerged from prison, blinking in the sunlight. The war was over, and they had been freed. But they would be taking their first steps in, and toward, freedom in a world that had changed beyond recognition.

7

"A Tryst with Destiny": 1945–1947

The British had not covered themselves with glory during the war. They had run a military dictatorship in a country that they had claimed to be preparing for democracy. They had presided over one of the worst famines in human history, the Great Bengal Famine of 1943, while diverting food (on Churchill's personal orders) from starving civilians to well-supplied Tommies. (Tens of thousands of Bengalis perished, but Churchill's only response to a telegram from the government in Delhi about the famine was to ask peevishly why Gandhi hadn't died yet.) Even Lord Wavell, who had been rewarded for military failure (in both the deserts of North Africa and the jungles of Burma) by succeeding Linlithgow as viceroy, considered the British government's attitude to India "negligent, hostile and contemptuous to a degree I had not anticipated."

Upon his release from prison Jawaharlal gave vent to his rage in such intemperate terms — at one point accusing members of the Viceroy's Executive Council of corruption — that he was very nearly arrested again. The Labour victory in the British general elections meant that the egregious Churchill was soon to be replaced as prime minister by Attlee, but this did not bring about any change in the anti-Congressism of the British authorities in India. Wavell convened a conference in Simla from late June 1945 (to which Jawaharlal, who held no major post in Congress, was not invited) which the viceroy allowed Jinnah to wreck. In this atmosphere of frustration and despair, the British called elections in India at the end of 1945, with the same franchise arrangements as in 1937, for seats in the central and provincial assemblies.

The Congress was woefully unequipped to contest them. Their blunder in surrendering the reins of power in 1939 and then losing their leadership and cadres to prison from 1942 meant that they went into the campaign tired, dispirited, and ill-organized. The League, on the other hand, had flourished during the war; its political machinery was well-oiled with patronage and pelf, while the Congress's was rusty from disuse. The electoral fortunes of 1937 were now significantly reversed. The Congress still carried a majority of the provinces. But except for the North-West Frontier Province, where the Congress won nineteen Muslim seats to the League's seventeen, the League swept the reserved seats for Muslims across the board, even in provinces like Bombay and Madras which had seemed immune to the communal contagion. Whatever the explanation — and Jawaharlal could have offered a few — there was no longer any escaping the reality that Jinnah and the Muslim League could now legitimately claim a popular mandate to speak for the majority of India's Muslims.

Jawaharlal did not believe this to mean that the partition of the country, which he thought totally impractical, was inevitable. In speeches, interviews, and articles throughout late 1945 and early 1946, he expressed the belief that, free of foreign rule, the Muslims of India would relinquish any thought of secession. The Muslims of India, he wrote, "are only technically a minority. They are vast in numbers and powerful in other ways, and it is patent that they cannot be coerced against their will. . . . This communal question is essentially one of protection of vested interests, and religion has always been a useful stalking horse for this purpose." He even argued that the Congress should grant the right of secession just to allay any Muslim fears, not in the expectation that the Muslim League–ruled provinces would actually exercise it. But whether, as many Indian analysts have suggested, Jinnah had really meant to establish a separate state or was merely advocating Pakistan to obtain leverage over the Congress, his followers had taken him at his word. A state of their own was what they were determined to have, and by the spring of 1946 Jawaharlal's idealism appeared naive, even dangerously so.

Divide et impera had worked too well. A device to maintain the integrity of British India had made it impossible for that integrity to be maintained without the British.

The British hold on the country was slipping. Even soldiers and policemen openly expressed their support for the nationalist leaders, heedless of the reaction of their British officers. Mutinies broke out in the air force and the British Indian navy. Violence erupted at political events. The demand for freedom was all but drowned out by the clamor for partition.

In a gesture so counterproductive that it might almost have been an act of expiation, the Raj clumsily gave the warring factions a last chance at unity. It decided to prosecute the defectors of Bose's Indian National Army. Bose himself had died in a fiery plane crash at war's end in Formosa, so the Raj sought to find scapegoats among his lieutenants. In a desire to appear evenhanded, the British chose to place three INA soldiers on trial in Delhi's historic Red Fort: a Hindu, a Muslim, and a Sikh. The result was a national outcry that spanned the communal divide. Whatever the errors and misjudgments of the INA men (and Jawaharlal believed freedom could never have come through an alliance with foreigners, let alone foreign Fascists), they had not been disloyal to their motherland. Each of the three defendants became a symbol of his community's proud commitment to independence from alien rule. Both the Congress and the League rose to the trio's defense; for the first time in their long careers, Jawaharlal and Jinnah accepted the same brief, Nehru donning a barrister's gown after twenty-five years.

But the moment passed: the defense of three patriots was no longer enough to guarantee a common definition of patriotism. The ferment across the country made the result of the trials almost irrelevant. The trials were eventually abandoned, because by the time they had begun it was apparent that the ultimate treason to the British Raj was being contemplated in its own capital. London, under the Labour Party, exhausted by war, was determined to rid itself of the burdens of its Indian empire. In February 1946, Prime Minister Attlee announced the dispatch of a Cabinet Mission to India "to discuss with leaders of Indian opinion the framing of an Indian Constitution." The endgame had begun.

Before the arrival of the Mission, Jawaharlal indulged his internationalist interests with a visit to Singapore and Malaya (with an unscheduled stop in Burma on the way back, where a weather delay enabled him to thwart the British and meet the Burmese nationalist hero Aung San). Permission to visit had initially been denied, then extended with humiliating conditions which he had declined to accept, but these had been overruled by the Supreme Commander for Asia himself, Lord Mountbatten. When he arrived in Singapore in March 1946 Nehru was welcomed with honors worthy of a head of government. Mountbatten received him personally and drove him to a canteen for Indian soldiers, where he was mobbed by the admiring men in uniform. Looking around for his hostess, Jawaharlal found Edwina Mountbatten crawling out from under the crowd; she had been knocked to the floor in the mad rush to greet him. It was, he later recalled, an unusual introduction. It was to become an unusual friendship.

The status Mountbatten chose to accord Jawaharlal was not accidental. It was clear he was India's man of destiny at a time when India's destiny was about to be realized. In early 1942 Mahatma Gandhi had told the Congress that there was no truth in the rumors that Nehru and he were estranged or that the more conservative Rajagopalachari, whose daughter had married one of the Mahatma's sons, was Gandhi's preferred successor. Jawaharlal liked to claim that he and the Mahatma spoke different languages, but "language," the Mahatma said, "is no bar to a union of hearts. And . . . when I am gone, [Nehru] will speak my language." The shrewd Gandhi had nurtured his protégé's leadership claims, engineering his ascent three times to the Congress's presidency. He knew that Jawaharlal had adopted him as a father figure, and if he was not always a faithful Gandhian, he would never fail to be a dutiful son.

In April 1946 Maulana Azad, after an unprecedented six years as Congress president, announced that he would be resigning and handing the reins to Jawaharlal. Sardar Patel and Acharya Kripalani, the Congress's general secretary, announced their candidacies as well, but the Mahatma intervened swiftly and decisively, and both men withdrew. On May 9, Kripalani announced that Jawaharlal Nehru had been elected unopposed as president of the Congress. Gandhi had managed to arrange his protégé's triumph at the most crucial time of all, with rumors of an interim Indian government being formed in advance of talks with the Cabinet Mission in Simla in May.

The Mission, a triumvirate of Sir Stafford Cripps (now the president of the Board of Trade), the British secretary of state for India, Lord Pethick-Lawrence, and

First Lord of the Admiralty A. V. Alexander, had arrived on March 24. The vultures, scenting the dying emanations of the Raj, began gathering for the kill. The negotiations and confabulations, intrigue and maneuvering among and within the various interested parties — the British, the Congress, the Muslim League, the Hindu Mahasabha, the loyalists, the Communists, the civil servants — became more intense and more convoluted with each passing day. Wavell's astonishingly candid diaries reveal his distaste for, and distrust of, practically every Indian politician he had to deal with, each (in his eyes) proving more dishonest than the next. Though he was, like most of the British administration, hostile to the Congress and sympathetic to the League his government had helped nurture, he was scathing in his contempt for the mendacity of the League's leaders, and of their "hymn of hate against Hindus." (No Congress leader expressed any hatred of Muslims to the viceroy.) Even the idea of Pakistan seemed to take many forms in the minds of its own advocates, with several seeing it as a Muslim state within a united India, and others advocating assorted forms of decentralized confederation rather than outright secession. (The American journalist Phillips Talbot recalls Sir Abdullah Haroon of the League showing him, in 1940, eight separate plans for Pakistan then being debated by the League's High Command.) Jinnah was steadfast in his demand for a separate state in the northwest and east of the country, but avoided giving specific answers as to how the creation of such a state could serve its declared purpose of protecting Muslims in the Hindu-majority provinces. Jawaharlal, meanwhile, sought nothing less than an Act of Abdication from the British: India's political arrangements should, he declared, be left to Indians to determine in their own Constituent Assembly, free of British mediation.

Part of the problem at the time may well have lain in a profound miscalculation on Jawaharlal's part about the true intentions of the British. Cut off by imprisonment from the political realities of world affairs, Nehru came to Simla believing (as he asserted to Phillips Talbot) that perfidious Albion was still trying to hold on to the jewel in her imperial crown by encouraging division among the Indian parties. Talbot felt that Nehru had simply not realized that Britain was exhausted, near-bankrupt, unwilling and unable to dispatch the sixty thousand British troops the government in London estimated would be required to reassert its control in India. London wanted to cut and run, and if the British could not leave behind a united India, they were prepared to "cut" the country quite literally before running. Nehru, still imagining an all-powerful adversary seeking to perpetuate its hegemony, and unaware of the extent to which the League had become a popular party among Indian Muslims, dealt with both on erroneous premises. "How differently would Nehru and his colleagues have negotiated," Talbot wondered, "had they understood Britain's weakness rather than continuing to be obsessed with its presumed strength?" The question haunts our hindsight.

When the Simla Conference began on May 9, 1946, Jinnah — who was cool but civil to Nehru — refused to shake hands with either of the two Muslim leaders of the Congress party, Azad and Abdul Ghaffar Khan; he wished to be seen as the sole spokesman of Muslim India. Nonetheless, when the Cabinet Mission proposed a three-tier plan for India's governance, with a weak center (limited to defense, external affairs, and communications), autonomous provinces (with the right of secession after five years), and groups of provinces (at least one of which would be predominantly Muslim), the League accepted the proposal, even though it meant giving up the idea of a sovereign Pakistan. The viceroy, without waiting for the Congress's formal acceptance of the scheme, invited fourteen Indians to serve as an interim government. While most of the leading Muslim Leaguers and Congressmen were on the list, there was a startling omission: not a single Muslim Congressman had been invited to serve. The Congress replied that it accepted the plan in principle, but could not agree to a government whose Muslim members were all from the League. Jinnah made it clear he could not accept anything else, and the resultant impasse proved intractable. The Cabinet Mission left for London with its plan endorsed but this dispute unresolved, leaving a caretaker Viceroy's Council in charge of the country. Ironically, its only Indian member (along with seven Englishmen) was a Muslim civil servant, Sir Akbar Hydari, who had made clear his fundamental opposition in principle to the idea of Pakistan.

Typically, Jawaharlal did not wait for the standoff to be resolved before plunging into another political crisis that brought into sharp relief both his opposition to communalism and his fierce republicanism. This was in the "princely state" of Kashmir, a Muslim-majority principality nominally outside the British Raj, whose autocratic and sybaritic Hindu maharajah Jawaharlal despised, and whose indigenous opposition, the noncommunal National Conference, was led by a friend and supporter, the Muslim socialist Sheikh Abdullah. Abdullah was president of the All-India States People's Conference, the Nehru-inspired assembly of antimonarchical nationalists who sought to merge their destinies with the rest of the Indian people by overthrowing the British puppets who ruled them in their nominally independent "princely states." Abdullah was on his way to Delhi to meet Jawaharlal in May 1946 when the maharajah had him arrested. Nehru (who nearly stormed out of Simla when he heard the news of Abdullah's arrest) protested vigorously to the British, and when this seemed to have had no effect, decided in mid-June to travel to Kashmir himself to assist in Abdullah's defense. On June 19 Jawaharlal was stopped at the border of the state by the Kashmiri authorities and served an "externment order." Jawaharlal erupted in anger at this treatment and, after five hours of waiting for the order to be reversed, defied it and crossed the state border anyway, whereupon he was promptly arrested. The British refused to press the maharajah to compromise, and the episode only ended when the Abdullah trial was adjourned and the Congress Working Committee asked Jawaharlal to return to Delhi.

On the face of it this was a trivial matter, but it showed Jawaharlal at his best — and his worst. The defense of principle at the risk of his personal freedom, and his loyalty to his friend and comrade, revealed the best of Jawaharlal, but they were accompanied by an impetuousness, and a tendency to fly into a rage at the slightest provocation, which did him less credit. There was also a touch of vainglory in his declaration at the border that

> During the past twenty-five years I have never obeyed a single order of the British Government in India or any Maharajah which came in my way. . . . When once a course of action is taken Jawaharlal never goes back, he goes forward; if you think otherwise then you don't know Jawaharlal. No power on earth can prevent me from going anywhere in India unless I am arrested or forcibly removed.

That was all very well, but indeed he was arrested, and it is unclear what good his defiance had done either for his cause or his friend. The nationalist movement's politics of protest had made Jawaharlal a master of the futile gesture — precisely the kind of politics that had led to the resignations of the Congress ministries in 1939 and the Quit India movement in 1942, and thus paved the way for the triumph of the Muslim League.

Meanwhile the problem of the Cabinet Mission's proposed government remained to be addressed. Both Congress and the League had accepted the plan in principle; the details were yet to be agreed upon. Jawaharlal, newly restored to the presidency of the Congress, chaired a meeting of the All-India Congress Committee in Bombay at which he rashly interpreted the Congress's acceptance of the plan as meaning that "We are not bound by a single thing except that we have decided to go into the Constituent Assembly." The implications of his statement were still being parsed when he repeated it at a press conference immediately afterward, adding that "we are absolutely free to act." Nehru stated specifically that he did not think the grouping of provinces, so important to the League, would necessarily survive a free vote. An incensed Jinnah reacted by withdrawing the League's acceptance of the Cabinet Mission Plan.

Jawaharlal was widely blamed for his thoughtlessness in provoking the end of the brief hope of Congress-League cooperation in a united Indian government, even on the League's terms. Patel was scathing, in a private letter, about Jawaharlal's "acts of emotional insanity" and "childlike innocence, which puts us all in great difficulties quite unexpectedly." Nehru "feels lonely and he acts emotionally," he wrote; ". . . he is impatient." Azad himself wrote in his memoirs that Nehru had been "carried away by his feelings" and "is so impressed by theoretical considerations that he is apt to underestimate the realities of a situation."

Had Jawaharlal held his tongue in July 1946, though, it is by no means clear that a common Congress-League understanding would have survived. Azad had been willing to relinquish the claims of Muslim Congressmen to office in the interests of unity, but the party as a whole was not prepared to concede the point to Jinnah. In stating that the grouping of provinces was not immutable, Jawaharlal was echoing the letter of the plan if not its spirit. (The League could have been accused of doing the same thing when it declared that the plan gave it the basis to work for Pakistan.) To see him as wrecker-in-chief of the country's last chance at avoiding partition is, therefore, to overstate the case. As his biographer M. J. Akbar put it, "Pakistan was created by Jinnah's will and Britain's willingness," not by Nehru's willfulness.

There was another consideration in Jawaharlal's mind when he spoke. His remarks were aimed at making the point that India's future as a sovereign independent state would depend on what Indians agreed to in a constituent assembly, not on what proposals the British got them to accept. Once again he had placed the larger principle over the immediate practical circumstance. Another politician might have considered it expedient to inveigle the League into the Constituent Assembly on the basis of the British proposals, but Jawaharlal scorned such tactics as beneath him. He later reacted to the posthumous publication of Azad's memoirs by suggesting that to blame him was to place too much importance on an individual rather than upon the forces of history. This very comment was, of course, confirmation of what his critics said of him: it was typical of Jawaharlal to dismiss a political argument with a theoretical proposition.

On August 8, 1946, the Congress Working Committee, bolstered by the admission of fresh faces appointed by the new president (including two relatively youthful women), declared that it accepted the Cabinet Mission Plan with its own interpretations on issues of detail. But this was not enough to bring Jinnah back into the game. Jawaharlal met with him (at Jinnah's home in Bombay) to seek agreement on an interim government, but Jinnah proved obdurate: he was determined to obtain Pakistan. The Muslim League leader declared August 16, 1946, as "Direct Action Day" to drive home this demand.

Thousands of Muslim Leaguers took to the streets in an orgy of violence, looting, and mayhem, and sixteen thousand innocents were killed in the resulting clashes, particularly in Calcutta. The police and army stood idly by: it seemed the British had decided to leave Calcutta to the mobs. Three days of communal rioting in the city left death and destruction in their wake before the army finally stepped in. But the carnage and hatred had also ripped apart something indefinable in the national psyche. Reconciliation now seemed impossible.

Yet a week later Wavell and Nehru were discussing the composition of an interim government for India, to consist of five "Caste Hindus," five Muslims, a "Scheduled Caste" member (one of those formerly known as "Untouchables"), and three minority representatives. They agreed that Jinnah could nominate his representatives but could have no say in the Congress's nominations — including, in principle, of a nationalist Muslim. Though the League was still deliberating about whether to join, an interim government of India was named, and its Congress members sworn in, on September 2, 1946. Jawaharlal was vice president of the Executive Council (presided over by the viceroy himself) and was assigned the portfolios of external and Commonwealth relations. In a broadcast on September 7 he seemed to view this as the culmination of a long struggle: "Too long have we been passive spectators of events, the playthings of others. The initiative comes to our people now and we shall make the history of our choice."

Jawaharlal was quick to assert his authority and that of his ministers, speaking out both on issues of procedure (sharply restricting the viceroy's authority to deal directly with matters that now belonged to the interim government) and substance (the situation in the princely states and the conduct of the British governors in the provinces). But the British remained supportive of the League and of its government in Bengal, which had allowed the horrors of Direct Action Day to occur. "What is the good of our forming the Interim Government of India," Nehru wrote indignantly to Wavell about conditions in Bengal in the wake of the Calcutta killings, "if all that we can do is to watch helplessly and do nothing else when thousands of people are being butchered . . . ?" But he went too far in insisting upon visiting the overwhelmingly Muslim, though Congress-ruled, North-West Frontier Province. The British connived in League-organized demonstrations against him at which stones were flung and Nehru was bruised. More important, the fiasco suggested that Nehru, as a Hindu, could never be acceptable to the province's Muslims as a national leader.

Meanwhile, British pressure on the Congress to make more concessions to Jinnah in order to secure the League's entry into the interim government prompted Gandhi and Nehru to relinquish voluntarily their right to nominate a Muslim member. This had been a deal-breaker for Jinnah, and he now seemed ready, in discussions with Jawaharlal, to find a compromise. But after their talks had made headway, Jinnah once again insisted that the Congress recognize the League as the sole representative of Indian Muslims. Jawaharlal refused to do this, saying it would be tantamount to a betrayal of the many nationalist Muslims in the Congress, and a stain on his own as well as the country's honor. The viceroy thereupon went behind the Congress's back and negotiated directly with Jinnah, accepting his nominations of Muslims as well as of a Scheduled Caste member. On October 15 the Muslim League formally announced that it would join the interim government.

But the League had done so only to wreck it from within. Even before its nominees were sworn in on October 26, they had made speeches declaring their real intention to be to work for the creation of Pakistan. The League's members met by themselves separately prior to each cabinet meeting and functioned in cabinet as an opposition group rather than as part of a governing coalition. On every issue, from the most trivial to the most important, the League members sought to obstruct the government's functioning, opposing every Congress initiative or proposal. Meanwhile, the League continued to instigate violence across the country; as riots broke out in Bihar in early November (with the Mahatma walking through the strife-torn province single-handedly restoring calm), Jinnah declared on November 14 that the killing would not stop unless Pakistan was created. The British convened talks in London in December to press the Congress to make further concessions to the League in order to persuade it to attend the Constituent Assembly. Jawaharlal, still burned by the reaction to his Bombay press conference, was at his most conciliatory, but Jinnah saw in the British position confirmation that his party's fortunes were in the ascendant, and escalated his demands. To Jawaharlal it seemed the British had learned nothing from the failure of the policy of appeasement in Europe in the 1930s.

The Constituent Assembly met as scheduled on December 9, without League participation, but was careful not to take any decisions that might alienate Jinnah. Nonetheless, on January 29, 1947, the Muslim League Working Committee passed a resolution asking the British government to declare that the Cabinet Mission Plan had failed, and to dissolve the Assembly. The Congress members of the interim government in turn demanded that the League members, having rejected the plan, resign. Amid the shambles of their policy, the British government announced that they would withdraw from India, come what may, no later than June 1948, and that to execute the transfer of power, Wavell would be replaced by the blue-blooded former Supreme Commander for Asia, Lord Mountbatten.

It was now increasingly apparent even to Jawaharlal that Pakistan, in some form, would have to be created; the League was simply not going to work with the Congress in a united government of India. He nonetheless tried to prod leaders of the League into discussions on the new arrangements, which he still hoped would fall short of an absolute partition. By early March, as communal rioting continued across northern India, even this hope had faded. Both Patel and Nehru agreed that, despite the Mahatma's refusal to contemplate such a prospect, the Congress had no alternative but to agree to partition Punjab and Bengal; the option of a loose Indian union including a quasi-sovereign Pakistan would neither be acceptable to the League nor result in a viable government for the rest of India. By the time Mountbatten arrived on March 24, 1947 the die had been cast. It was he, however, who rapidly ended the game altogether.

Mountbatten later claimed he governed by personality, and indeed both his positive and negative attributes would prove decisive. On the one hand he was focused, energetic, charming, and free of racial bias, unlike almost every one of his predecessors; on the other, he was astonishingly vain, alarmingly impatient, and easily swayed by personal likes and dislikes. His vicereine, Edwina, was a vital partner, one who took a genuine interest in Indian affairs. Theirs was a curious marriage, marked by her frequent infidelities, which he condoned, and it has been suggested that her affection for Jawaharlal played a part in some of his (and Mountbatten's) decisions relating to Indian independence. There is no question that Jawaharlal and Edwina indeed became close, and some circumstantial evidence that they may well have become closer at a later stage in their lives, but it does not seem likely that this occurred early enough to have any political impact (or indeed that, if it did, it would have had any political impact). Nehru was certainly no celibate; particularly after the death of Kamala when he was only forty-seven, he enjoyed close relations with a number of women friends, though he never contemplated marriage again. Nehru's biographer Frank Moraes wrote that Edwina "sensed that what Nehru most wanted and did not know how to achieve was to relax." This she was able to get him to do, at a time of great tension. But while he enjoyed Edwina's company, he had far more on his mind in 1947 than a dalliance with the viceroy's spouse.

For one thing, India was aflame; for another, it stood on the brink of a new dawn, one that would, in Jawaharlal's view, enable it to play a great role in world affairs. Nehru was therefore instrumental in convening the

Asian Relations Conference in New Delhi in March 1947, attended by delegates, officials, and scholars of almost every conceivable shade of Asian opinion, including representatives of the Chinese Communists and the Kuomintang, of Soviet Central Asia and British Malaya, of the Arab League and the Hebrew University (and even of Egypt, despite the geographical anomaly of its presence at an Asian gathering), but not of Japan, whose invitees were denied exit permits by the American occupying forces. The USA, the USSR, Australia, New Zealand, and Britain sent observers, who heard Jawaharlal declaim at the opening: "Standing on this watershed which divides two epochs of human history and endeavor, we can look back on our long past and look forward to the future that is taking shape before our eyes. . . . For too long we of Asia have been petitioners in Western courts and chancelleries. That story must now belong to the past. We propose to stand on our own feet and to co-operate with all others who are prepared to cooperate with us." But even as he spoke, the country around him was consumed by violence, as the freedom struggle crumbled toward partition.

For Jawaharlal the conference marked "the beginnings of a new era in Asian history," though it is difficult, with hindsight, to see how. Certainly there were no follow-up conferences held, no pan-Asian institutions established. But perhaps it signaled the first articulation of a postcolonial consciousness which was later to find expression in the Bandung Afro-Asian Conference of 1955 and the Nonaligned movement. Asia as a political idea remained Jawaharlal's alone.

Meanwhile events at home were deteriorating.

Communal violence and killings were a daily feature; so was Jinnah's complete unwillingness to cooperate with the Congress on any basis other than that it represented the Hindus and he the Muslims of India. The British gave him much encouragement to pursue this position: the governor of the North-West Frontier Province, the pro-League Sir Olaf Caroe, was unconscionably pressing the Congress government of this Muslim-majority state to make way for the League, since its continuation would have made Pakistan impossible. As the impasse in the interim government continued, Mountbatten and his advisers drew up a "Plan Balkan" that would have transferred power to the provinces rather than to a central government, leaving them free to join a larger union (or not). The British kept Nehru in the dark while "Plan Balkan" was reviewed (and revised) in London. When he was finally shown the text by Mountbatten at Simla on the night of May 10, Jawaharlal erupted in indignation, storming into his friend Krishna Menon's[7] room at 2 A.M. to sputter his outrage. Had the plan been implemented, the idea of India that Jawaharlal had so brilliantly evoked in his writings would have been sundered even more comprehensively than Jinnah was proposing.

[7] V. K. Krishna Menon, an acerbic south Indian intellectual and longtime London resident, had helped publish Jawaharlal in England and led the pro-Congress India League since 1929. Jawaharlal met Menon for the first time in London in 1935 and was greatly impressed with his intelligence, his energy, and his left-wing credentials, but observed: "he has the virtues and failings of the intellectual." Their friendship was deep, abiding, and, as we shall see, ultimately ill-starred.

Balkanization would have unleashed civil war and disorder on an unimaginable scale, as provinces, princely states, and motley political forces contended for power upon the departure of the Raj.

A long, passionate, and occasionally incoherent note of protest from Jawaharlal to Mountbatten killed the plan. But the only alternative was partition. In May Jawaharlal saw the unrest in the country as "volcanic": the time had come for making hard and unpleasant choices, and he was prepared to make them. Reluctantly, he agreed to Mountbatten's proposal for a referendum in the North-West Frontier Province and in the Muslim-majority district of Sylhet, gave in on a Congress counterproposal for a similar approach in regard to Hindu-majority districts of Sind, and, most surprisingly, agreed to Dominion status for India. The Jawaharlal who agreed to Dominion status was the same man who had moved the independence resolution in Madras in 1927 and danced around the flagpole in Lahore two years later. In December 1946 he had proposed in the Constituent Assembly that India should be a sovereign democratic republic. Yet six months later he was willing to accept Dominion status for India within the British Commonwealth.

Some critics see in all this an exhausted Jawaharlal's anxiety to end the tension once and for all; others suggest that he allowed his regard for the Mountbattens to trump his own principles (and some wonder whether Edwina played a part in bringing about the series of concessions). Such arguments do a great disservice to Jawaharlal Nehru. His correspondence at the time shows a statesman in great anguish trying to do the best for his country when all other options had failed. As long as the British gave Jinnah a veto over every proposal he found uncongenial, there was little else Nehru could do. Nor is there evidence in the writings and reflections of the other leading Indian nationalists of the time that any of them had any better ideas. The only exception was Gandhi: the Mahatma went to Mountbatten and suggested that India could be kept united if Jinnah were offered the leadership of the whole country. Jawaharlal and Patel both gave that idea short shrift, and Mountbatten did not seem to take it seriously.

There is no doubt that Mountbatten seemed to proceed with unseemly haste, and that in so doing he swept the Indian leaders along. Nehru was convinced that Jinnah was capable of setting the country ablaze and destroying all that the nationalist movement had worked for: a division of India was preferable to its destruction. "It is with no joy in my heart that I commend these proposals," Nehru told his party, "though I have no doubt in my mind that it is the right course." The distinction between heart and head was poignant, and telling. On June 3, Jawaharlal, Jinnah, and the Sikh leader Baldev Singh broadcast news of their acceptance of partition to the country. The occasion again brought out the best in Jawaharlal:

> We are little men serving a great cause, but because that cause is great something of that greatness falls upon us also. Mighty forces are at work in the world today and in India. . . . [It is my hope] that in this way we shall reach that united India sooner than

> otherwise and that she will have a stronger and more secure foundation. . . . The India of geography, of history and tradition, the India of our minds and hearts, cannot change.

But of course it could change: geography was to be hacked, history misread, tradition denied, minds and hearts torn apart. Jawaharlal imagined that the rioting and violence that had racked the country over the League's demand for Pakistan would die down once that demand had been granted, but he was wrong. The killing and mass displacement worsened as people sought frantically to be on the "right" side of the lines the British were to draw across their homeland. Over a million people died in the savagery that bookended the freedom of India and Pakistan; some seventeen million were displaced, and countless properties destroyed and looted. Lines meant lives. What Jawaharlal had thought of as a temporary secession of certain parts of India hardened into the creation of two separate and hostile states that would fight three wars with each other over the next twenty-four years.

The Mahatma was not the only one to be assailed by a sense of betrayal. The Congress government in the North-West Frontier Province, let down by the national party, chose to boycott the referendum there, which passed with the votes of just 50.49 percent of the electorate (but nearly 99 percent of those who voted). Mountbatten, who had seen himself serving for a while as a bridge between the two new Dominions by holding the governor-generalship of both, was brusquely told by

Jinnah that the League leader himself would hold that office in Pakistan. The outgoing viceroy would therefore have to content himself with the titular overlordship of India alone.

On August 4 Jawaharlal sent Mountbatten the list of fourteen names he proposed for independent India's first cabinet. Patel would be his deputy and in charge of home affairs, bringing his considerable organizational skills to the calamitous law-and-order situation and to the integration of the princely states. The rest of the list was a remarkably impressive distillation of the best and the brightest of India's political elite, while ensuring regional and religious representation: four "Caste Hindus," including the Hindu Mahasabha leader Dr. Shyama Prasad Mookerji; two Muslims, Azad and Kidwai; the Sikh leader Baldev Singh; two Christians, one of whom was a princess of Sikh origin; two Scheduled Caste leaders, including the radical Ambedkar, who had so often been the Congress's nemesis; and a Parsi. The south of India had two representatives to the north's twelve — Rajagopalachari, a notable omission, was to be dispatched to strife-torn Bengal as governor — but this imbalance apart, Jawaharlal Nehru's first cabinet list set a standard that would never again be matched, while establishing a precedent for diversity that all his successors would strive to emulate.

A scurrilous rumor did the rounds that Nehru had initially omitted his main rival in the Congress, Sardar Patel, from the list and had been obliged by Mountbatten to include him. This was completely untrue. Though Patel had sought to challenge Jawaharlal's ascent in 1946, he understood why the Mahatma saw in the younger man a more plausible leader for all of India. In turn, Nehru, in inviting Patel to serve as his deputy, called him "the strongest pillar of the Cabinet." Patel replied: "My services will be at your disposal, I hope, for the rest of my life and you will have unquestioned loyalty and devotion from me in the cause for which no man in India has sacrificed as much as you have done. Our combination is unbreakable and therein lies our strength." The Sardar's assurances proved completely true, and their "combination" was indispensable as independent India found its feet. Sadly, though, the "rest of my life" that Patel alluded to would extend no more than another three years.

The man who, as Congress president in Lahore in 1929, had first demanded *purna swaraj* (full independence), now stood ready to claim it, even if the city in which he had moved his famous resolution was no longer to be part of the newly free country. Amid the rioting and carnage that consumed large sections of northern India, Jawaharlal Nehru found the time to ensure that no pettiness marred the moment: he dropped the formal lowering of the Union Jack from the independence ceremony in order not to hurt British sensibilities. The Indian tricolor was raised just before sunset, and as it fluttered up the flagpole a late-monsoon rainbow emerged behind it, a glittering tribute from the heavens. Just before midnight, Jawaharlal Nehru rose in the Constituent Assembly to deliver the most famous speech ever made by an Indian:

> Long years ago we made a tryst with destiny, and now the time comes when we shall redeem our

> pledge, not wholly or in full measure, but very substantially. At the stroke of the midnight hour, when the world sleeps, India will awake to life and freedom. A moment comes, which comes but rarely in history, when we step out from the old to the new, when an age ends, and when the soul of a nation long suppressed finds utterance.

"This is no time . . . for ill-will or blaming others," he added. "We have to build the noble mansion of free India where all her children may dwell." And typically he ended this immortal passage with a sentence that combined both humility and ambition, looking beyond the tragedy besieging his moment of triumph to India's larger place in the world: "It is fitting," he said, "that at this solemn moment we take the pledge of dedication to the service of India and her people and to the still larger cause of humanity."

There would be challenges enough ahead, but Jawaharlal Nehru would never cease, even at the moment of his greatest victory, to look above the suffering around him and fix his gaze upon a distant dream.

8

"Commanding Heights": 1947–1957

One man did not join the celebrations that midnight. Mahatma Gandhi stayed in Calcutta, fasting, striving to keep the peace in a city that just a year earlier had been ravaged by killing. He saw no cause for celebration. Instead of the cheers of rejoicing, he heard the cries of the women ripped open in the internecine frenzy; instead of the slogans of freedom, he heard the shouts of the crazed assaulters firing their weapons at helpless refugees, and the silence of trains arriving full of corpses massacred on their journey; instead of the dawn of Jawaharlal's promise, he saw only the long dark night of horror that was breaking his country in two. In his own Independence Day message to the nation Jawaharlal could not help thinking of the Mahatma:

> On this day, our first thoughts go to the architect of freedom, the Father of our Nation who, embodying the old spirit of India, held aloft the torch. . . . We have often been unworthy followers of his, and we have strayed from his message, but not only we, but the succeeding generations, will remember his message and bear the imprint in their hearts.

It was a repudiation as well as a tribute: the Mahatma was now gently relegated to the "old spirit of India" from whom the custodians of the new had "strayed." In his crushing disillusionment with his own people (of all religions), the Mahatma announced that he would spend the rest of his years in Pakistan, a prospect that made the leaders of the League collectively choke. But he never got there: on January 30, 1948, a Hindu extremist angered by Gandhi's sympathy for Muslims shot him dead after a prayer meeting. Mahatma Gandhi died with the name of God on his lips.

The grieving nation found grim solace only in the fact that his assassin had been a Hindu, not a Muslim; the retaliatory rage that a Muslim killer would have provoked against his coreligionists would have made the partition riots look like a school-yard brawl. "The light has gone out of our lives," a brokenhearted Jawaharlal declared in a moving broadcast to the nation, "and there is darkness everywhere. . . . The light has gone out, I said, and yet I was wrong. . . . For that light represented something more than the immediate present; it represented the living truth, the eternal truths, reminding us of the right path, drawing us from error, taking this ancient country to freedom." Jawaharlal Nehru had lost a father figure; after Motilal's death he had grown at the feet of the Mahatma, relying on the older man's wisdom, advice, and patronage. Now, at the age of fifty-eight, he was truly alone.

The first months of independence were anything but easy. Often emotional, Jawaharlal was caught up in the human drama of the times. He was seen weeping at the sight of a victim one day, and erupting in rage at a would-be assailant hours later. Friends thought his physical health would be in danger as he stormed from city to village, ordering his personal bodyguards to shoot any Hindu who might attack a Muslim, providing refuge in his own home in Delhi for Muslims terrified for their lives, giving employment to young refugees who had lost everything. The American editor Norman Cousins recounted how one night in August Hindu rioters in New Delhi, "inflamed by stories of Moslem terror . . . smashed their way into Moslem stores, destroying and looting and ready to kill":

> Even before the police arrived in force, Jawaharlal Nehru was on the scene . . . , trying to bring people to their senses. He spied a Moslem who had just been seized by Hindus. He interposed himself between the man and his attackers. Suddenly a cry went up: "Jawaharlal is here!" . . . It had a magical effect. People stood still. . . . Looted merchandise was dropped. The mob psychology disintegrated. By the time the police arrived people were dispersing. The riot was over. . . . The fact that Nehru had

> risked his life to save a single Moslem had a profound effect far beyond New Delhi. Many thousands of Moslems who had intended to flee to Pakistan now stayed in India, staking their lives on Nehru's ability to protect them and assure them justice.

Affairs of state were just as draining. The new prime minister of India had to deal with the consequences of the carnage sweeping the country; preside over the integration of the princely states into the Indian Union; settle disputes with Pakistan on issues involving the division of finances, of the army, and of territory; cope with massive internal displacement, as refugees thronged Delhi and other cities; keep a fractious and divided nation together; and define both a national and an international agenda. On all issues but that of foreign policy, he relied heavily on Patel, who welded the new country together with formidable political and administrative skills and a will of iron. A more surprising ally was the former viceroy, now governor-general of India, Lord Mountbatten.

For all his culpability in rushing India to an independence drenched in blood, Mountbatten made Nehru partial amends by staying on in India for just under a year. As heir to a British government whose sympathy for the League had helped it carve out a country from the collapse of the Raj, Mountbatten enjoyed a level of credibility with the rulers of Pakistan that no Indian governor-general could have had. This made him a viable and impartial interlocutor with both sides at a time of great tension. When fighting broke out over Kashmir between the two Dominions (whose armies were still each commanded by a British general), Mountbatten helped prevent a deeper engagement by the Pakistani army and brought about an end to the war. Equally, as a governor-general above the political fray, he played a crucial role in persuading maharajahs and nawabs distrustful of the socialist Nehru to accept that they had no choice but to merge their domains into the Indian Union. And the governor-general and his wife distinguished themselves by their personal interest in and leadership of the emergency relief measures that saved millions of desperate refugees from misery and worse. In 1950, when India became a republic with its own Constitution, Jawaharlal arranged for it to remain within the British Commonwealth, acknowledging the British sovereign no longer as head of state but as the symbol of the free association of nations who wished to retain a British connection. Mountbatten's influence was decisive in prompting Jawaharlal to make this choice. Nehru's close relations with Edwina Mountbatten have been the stuff of much posthumous gossip, but his relationship with her husband was to have the more lasting impact on India's history.

As prime minister, Jawaharlal had ultimate responsibility for many of the decisions taken during the tense period from 1947 to 1949, but it is true to say he was still finding his feet as a governmental leader and that on many key issues he simply went along with what Patel and Mountbatten wanted. Nehru was the uncontested voice of Indian nationalism, the man who had "discovered" India in his own imagination, but he could not build the India of his vision without help. When the

Muslim rulers of Hindu-majority Junagadh and Hyderabad, both principalities surrounded by Indian territory, flirted with independence (in Hyderabad's case) and accession to Pakistan (in Junagadh's), the Indian army marched in and took over with scarcely a shot being fired. In both cases the decision was Patel's, with acquiescence from Nehru. When the Hindu maharajah of Jammu and Kashmir tried to postpone a decision to accede to either India or Pakistan and found his state invaded by Pathan "irregulars" from Pakistan, it was Mountbatten who insisted on accession to India as a precondition for sending in the army to resist the invaders. Nehru, confident in the support of Kashmiri public opinion as manifest in the support of the secular nationalist Sheikh Abdullah, made accession conditional upon a reference to the will of the people: it was Jawaharlal's proposal that a plebiscite be held immediately to ascertain their wishes. But when the Pakistani army joined the fray, and as the military tide turned in India's favor, it was Mountbatten who prevailed upon Nehru, against Patel's advice, to declare a cease-fire and take the dispute to the United Nations.

From the Indian nationalist point of view this was a gross error, since it converted what was thus far a domestic Indian problem into an international dispute. Jawaharlal's decision to appeal to the UN has been seen within the country as a blunder that snatched diplomatic stalemate from the jaws of imminent military victory. But this is unreasonable; after all, Pakistan could just as easily have raised the issue at the UN, and it would have found some support. Recent scholarship has confirmed that British diplomacy at the time played a particularly active role in recasting the issue internationally to India's disadvantage. Jawaharlal saw that policy considerations going well beyond Kashmir — including the West's general desire to improve its standing in the Islamic world amid trauma in Palestine, and the potential usefulness of Pakistan as an advocate for Britain with the Arab countries — influenced London's actions. But Nehru should hardly have been surprised to see other countries acting in pursuit of their own interests: the wonder was that a man of such sharp intelligence and insight should have failed to more clearly define and act upon India's.

By August 1953 Jawaharlal's Kashmir policy was in a shambles. His friend and ally Sheikh Abdullah had begun flirting with notions of independence, and Nehru made the painful decision to place him under arrest. A compliant pro-Congress politician replaced Abdullah, but the development changed the complexion of the Kashmir dispute, on which international opinion was now broadly ranged against India. Domestically Jawaharlal was criticized for granting Jammu and Kashmir a special constitutional status — prohibiting non-Kashmiris from buying land in the state, for example, a provision which made it impossible to resettle refugees from Pakistan there. Abroad, the dispute Nehru had first internationalized now hung over India's head like the proverbial sword of Damocles, and the issue of Kashmir continued to bedevil relations with Pakistan throughout Jawaharlal's tenure — and beyond.

Apart from handling weighty matters of state, Jawaharlal had to deal with issues of domestic politics. He had surprised some of his most ardent supporters by his reluctance to embrace radical change, and his willingness to retain, and indeed rely on, the very civil servants and armed services personnel who had served the British Raj, the "steel frame" of which continued as the administrative superstructure of independent India. The government proved its worth in handling the rehabilitation of some seven million refugees from Pakistan, a colossal political and administrative feat. But the civil service continued in the traditions of colonial governance learned from their British masters; Nehru did little to instill in them a development orientation or a new ethic of service to the people. Continuity, not change, was the watchword. Many of the freedom fighters, who had gone to jail while these officials prospered under the British, were dismayed.

The Congress socialists, heirs to those who had found Jawaharlal insufficiently radical in the 1920s and 1930s, formally split from the parent party in March 1948. Nehru shared their ideals but was, in their view, in thrall to capitalist and right-wing forces; his ability to compromise, to work with those he had once denounced, even his eclectic cabinet which drew upon all shades of Indian opinion, were seen as proof that socialism would never come to India through him. Jawaharlal lamented their departure and particularly that of their leader, a figure of rare integrity and strength of character, Jayaprakash (JP) Narayan. Had the Congress divided completely on ideological lines, Jawaharlal might have belonged with them; but he was prime minister and leader of a party that had won India's freedom and still strived to represent the various currents of belief that had sustained this cause. Nehru sought instead to serve as a bridge between the two principal opposing forces within the Congress: the right, grouped around Patel and Rajendra Prasad, who were prepared to ban trade unions, woo the Hindu-nationalist Rashtriya Swayamsevak Sangh (RSS), dismiss Muslim officials, and promote the interests of the Hindu majority; and the socialist left whose policy prescriptions, in Jawaharlal's own words, "show an amazing lack of responsibility."

Ideology was not the only dividing issue; secularism was equally important. In resisting the anti-Muslim currents in his party that had come to the fore in the wake of partition, Jawaharlal recognized that Jinnah's triumph in creating a Muslim nation had weakened the case for secularism in India and increased communal feeling in the minds of politicians who had earlier considered themselves Gandhians. The steady influx of Hindu refugees from Pakistan hardened attitudes in India. Jawaharlal's correspondence in 1948 and 1949 shows him almost reduced to despair by the growth of anti-Muslim feeling — what he called the "refugee mentality." But he remained a staunch defender of the place of Muslims in a secular India, a position from which he never wavered either personally or politically. His idea of India explicitly rejected the two-nation theory; having spurned the logic which had created a state for Muslims, he was not about to succumb to the temptation of mirroring that logic by allowing India to become a state for Hindus. "So long as I am Prime minister," he declared in 1950, "I shall not allow communalism to shape our policy." And during the

1952 elections he declared to a large crowd in Old Delhi: "If any person raises his hand to strike down another on the ground of religion, I shall fight him till the last breath of my life, both at the head of the government and from outside."

Gandhi's assassination by a Hindu fanatic strengthened his hand on the communal issue. Even Patel agreed to the RSS being banned, though the ban was lifted after a year. On other questions, ranging from the grant of "privy purses" (annual subventions to the erstwhile maharajahs to compensate for the loss of their princely states) to the clash between the right to property and the need for land reform, he found himself outmaneuvered by the party's right wing. Patel ran his Home Ministry as firmly as he administered the country as a whole, and he brooked little interference from Nehru.

Lord Mountbatten left India for good on June 21, 1948, ten months after he had presided over its freedom — and its dismemberment. He was succeeded as governor-general of the Dominion by the man who had once been thought more likely than Jawaharlal to be Gandhi's heir, C. Rajagopalachari. Though temperamentally a conservative, "Rajaji" had no patience for the communal sympathies of the Congress right, and so in his own way complemented Jawaharlal as head of state. But when the time came for that position to be converted to that of president of the Republic (upon the adoption of independent India's new Constitution on the symbolic date of January 26, 1950, the old "Independence Day" becoming the new Republic Day), Patel engineered the election of his crony Rajendra Prasad as the Congress candidate. Jawaharlal had been completely bypassed; he was so surprised that he actually asked Prasad to withdraw and propose Rajagopalachari's name himself. Prasad cleverly suggested that he would do whatever Nehru and Patel agreed upon, at which point Nehru understood and threw in the towel. One of Prasad's first acts upon election was to ask that January 26 be changed to a date deemed more auspicious by his astrologers. Jawaharlal flatly turned him down, declaring that India would not be run by astrologers if he had anything to do with it. This time, Nehru won.

Nehru and Patel came dangerously close to a public clash only once. In 1950, under pressure from the right to intervene militarily in East Pakistan where a massacre of Hindus had begun, Jawaharlal first tried to work with his Pakistani counterpart, Liaquat Ali Khan, on a joint approach to communal disturbances, and then, when this had been ignored by Liaquat, offered President Prasad his resignation. (Stanley Wolpert has speculated that Jawaharlal, exhausted and heartsick, was contemplating eloping with Edwina Mountbatten, who had just been visiting him at the time.) But when Patel called a meeting of Congressmen at his home to criticize Jawaharlal's weakness on the issue, Nehru fought back, withdrawing his offer of resignation, challenging Patel to a public debate on Pakistan policy, and even writing to Patel to express doubt as to whether the two of them could work together anymore. The counter-assault was so ferocious that Patel backed off and affirmed his loyalty to Jawaharlal, supporting the pact Nehru signed with his Pakistani counterpart (which had even prompted the two cabinet ministers from Bengal to resign). The entire episode marked the closest the Congress would ever come to repudiating Nehru in his lifetime.

But in those early days Jawaharlal was not always a successful political infighter. His setback over Prasad's election was echoed in the elections to the Congress Party presidency a few months later. Having withdrawn from the race himself on the grounds that it would not be proper for him as prime minister to also serve as party president, Jawaharlal supported his old rival Kripalani against the rightist Purushottam Das Tandon (the very man whose inability to win Muslim support for the chairmanship of the Allahabad municipality had given Jawaharlal his experience of mayoralty in 1923). But Tandon had Patel's backing, and despite Jawaharlal's open opposition, won handily, with over 50 percent of the votes in a three-man field. Nehru publicly grumbled that the result would only please communal and reactionary forces in the country, and refused to join Tandon's Working Committee. When finally cajoled into doing so he made no secret of his reluctance. He spent the next year undermining Tandon much as his mentor Mahatma Gandhi had undermined Bose thirteen years earlier. In September 1951 Jawaharlal brought matters to a head by resigning his party positions and making it clear that he and Tandon could not coexist: one of them had to go. Tandon did. Jawaharlal himself was elected Congress president, his earlier scruples about the prime minister serving in such a position completely forgotten.

There was another reason for the decisiveness of his victory. By this time Nehru's greatest rival, Sardar Patel, was dead. He had a suffered a heart attack a few months after the Mahatma's assassination; then stomach cancer struck, and in December 1950, having fulfilled his historic role of consolidating India's fragile freedom, he passed away, aged seventy-six. Patel and Nehru had also served as a check upon each other, and his passing left Jawaharlal unchallenged. If ever there was a moment when he might have been tempted by the prospect of near-dictatorial authority, this might have been it, but Jawaharlal remained a convinced democrat. He was not, however, a naive one. He realized that the Home Ministry, with its control over the institutions of law and order, was a valuable tool for a potential competitor. He was therefore careful after the Sardar's death to appoint only trusted associates — with no competing political ambitions or agendas of their own — to the Home Ministry.

Jawaharlal's efforts to resist the right-wing tendencies within his party and government were not aided by the continuing departures of his socialist allies. JP Narayan's exit in 1948 was followed by Kripalani's and Kidwai's resignation from the Congress in 1951. Kidwai had been a vital Muslim ally in Uttar Pradesh and was a serving member of Nehru's cabinet when he left to join Kripalani in forming a left-wing party. But these desertions only made Jawaharlal more determined then ever to fight his corner. When President Prasad sought directly to send Parliament his objections to the Hindu Code Bill (an attempt to reform Hindu personal law that Jawaharlal was strongly promoting), Nehru told him this would be an unconstitutional interference in the work of his government and threatened to resign over the issue. Prasad backed off.

The death of Patel and the sidelining of Rajaji also had a negative consequence. They left Jawaharlal literally peerless. With neither Patel nor Rajaji present in the councils of state, Nehru was deprived of the critical support, companionship, and challenge of an equal — someone whose standing and experience in the nationalist movement was as great, and as long, as his own. No longer was there anyone within the government or the party leadership to contest his authority or judgment. From now on, India's triumphs and failures would rest on Jawaharlal's shoulders alone.

In October 1951 India began conducting its first general elections, a process that took six months, engaged 176 million voters (85 percent of whom were illiterate), and saw more than 17,000 candidates from 75 political parties contest 489 seats in the national Parliament and 3,375 in the various state assemblies. The event was unprecedented, since it extended the franchise (limited under British rule) to all adults and embarked the nation upon a remarkable process of political education in the promises and the pitfalls of democracy. At a time when independence and the violence of partition were still fresh in the minds of voters, Nehru stewarded his party and his people into their first full appreciation of the rights and privileges that came with their freedom. As in 1936 and 1946, he campaigned extensively, traveling 25,000 miles, though this time mostly by plane. The voter turnout was respectable at 60 percent, and the Congress won an absolute majority of seats nationally (364 of the 489 seats) and in 18 of the 25 states — but on the strength of only 45 percent of the vote in the Westminster-style first-past-the-post system. Yet the process of having to defend itself and its policies in the face of organized opposition was healthy for the party. It was also salutary for its critics: the Socialists, for instance, were decimated (but the Communists emerged as India's second-largest party). In his own constituency, Phulpur, Jawaharlal faced a Hindu sadhu who tried to exploit his coreligionists' disillusionment with Nehru's "appeasement" of Muslims. Nehru won by 233,571 votes to 56,718.

The general elections legitimized Congress rule and Jawaharlal Nehru's prime ministership of India. It was an India whose internal political contours he would soon have to change. During the nationalist movement the Congress had affirmed the principle of linguistic states, arguing that language was the only viable basis for India's political geography. But partition shocked Nehru (and Patel) into rejecting any proposal to redraw state boundaries, for fear of accelerating any latent fissiparous tendencies in the country. So independent India's provincial boundaries remained drawn for administrative convenience until a southern Gandhian, Potti Sriramulu, undertook a fast-unto-death for the creation of a Telugu-speaking Andhra state — and, after fifty-five days of fasting, actually died. Protests erupted throughout the Telugu-speaking districts of Madras, and Nehru gave in. Andhra Pradesh was created and a States' Reorganization Commission appointed, whose recommendation in 1955 to redraw India's internal boundaries along mainly linguistic lines was largely implemented the following year.

Meanwhile, Jawaharlal saw in his 1952 electoral

victory an affirmation of popular support for the principles of socialism and anti-imperialism that he had begun articulating publicly in the 1936 campaign. Though not formally a Marxist, Jawaharlal had revealed a susceptibility to Marxian analyses of historical forces in his early writings. In an unfinished review of Bertrand Russell's 1918 book *Roads to Freedom* Nehru had already laid out the basics of his political philosophy. "Present-day democracy," he wrote (in 1919), "manipulated by the unholy alliance of capital, property, militarism and an overgrown bureaucracy, and assisted by a capitalist press, has proved a delusion and a snare." But "Orthodox Socialism does not give us much hope. . . . [A]n all-powerful state is no lover of individual liberty. . . . Life under Socialism would be a joyless and soulless thing, regulated to the minutest detail by rules and orders." At the Lucknow Congress in 1936 Nehru had gone further, declaring: "I am convinced that the only key to the solution of the world's problems and of India's problems lies in socialism. . . . I see no way of ending the poverty, the vast unemployment, the degradation and the subjection of the Indian people except through socialism. That involves vast and revolutionary changes in our political and social structure, . . . a new civilization radically different from the present capitalist order. Some glimpse we can have of this new civilization in the territories of the USSR. . . . If the future is full of hope it is largely because of Soviet Russia."

But he came to temper that view: Nehru was too much of a Gandhian to be a fellow-traveler of the Soviet Union, though he shared the admiration for the triumphs of the 1917 Revolution commonly felt by leftists of his generation. But he always put nationalism before ideology: convinced that the Communists' loyalties were extraterritorial, he demanded of a band of Communists waving their hammer-and-sickle banner during the 1952 campaign, "Why don't you go and live in the country whose flag you are carrying?" (They replied, in staggering ignorance of their critic: "Why don't you go to New York and live with the Wall Street imperialists?")

Jawaharlal's constant search for the politically viable middle had kept him at the head of the eclectic Congress Party rather than led him to the ranks of his ideological soulmates, the Socialists. Nehruvian socialism was a curious amalgam of idealism (of a particularly English Fabian variety), a passionate if somewhat romanticized concern for the struggling masses (derived from his own increasingly imperial travels amid them), a Gandhian faith in self-reliance (learned at the spinning wheel and typified by the ostentatious wearing of khadi), a corollary distrust of Western capital (flowing from his elemental anticolonialism), and a "modern" belief in "scientific" methods like Planning (the capital letter is deliberate: Nehru elevated the technique to a dogma).

This idiosyncratic variant of socialism became an increasing hallmark of his rule. Jawaharlal saw Indian capitalism as weak and concentrated in a few hands; to him the state was the only guarantor of the economic welfare of ordinary people. Some degree of planning was probably unavoidable; even the Bombay business community drew up a plan in 1944 for India's rapid industrialization. There was certainly a need for the state to invest some resources where the private sector would not, particularly in infrastructure and in agriculture. The economist Jagdish Bhagwati has suggested that what India needed at the time was probably socialism on the land and capitalism in industry. Nehru tried the opposite. Despite Patel's skepticism, Nehru prompted the government of India to adopt an Industrial Policy Resolution in April 1948 that granted the state monopolies over railways, atomic energy, and defense manufacturing as well as reserved rights relating to any new enterprise in a host of vital areas, from coal and steel to shipbuilding and communications. The Constitution that came into force on January 29, 1950 included a section on the "Directive Principles of State Policy" which enshrined socialist goals but made them objectives, not enforceable rights. In 1950 the government of India created a permanent Planning Commission with Jawaharlal Nehru as chairman.

The result was to embark the nation upon a series of Five-Year Plans, starting in 1952, that bore successively decreasing relation to reality; actively impeded, rather than facilitated, the country's development; and shackled India to what became derisively known in economic circles as "the Hindu rate of growth" (a fitful 3 percent when the rest of the developing countries of Asia were racing along at 10 to 12 percent or better). Nehru's mistrust of foreign capital kept out much-needed foreign investment but paradoxically made India more dependent on foreign aid. This applied not just to industry: the First Plan's necessary emphasis on agriculture (essential following the loss of the "national granary," West Punjab, to Pakistan)

was so faulty in conception that by 1957 the country's agricultural output had dropped below that of 1953 and the government was soon importing food grains in a country where four out of five Indians scratched their living from the land.

Nehru's economic assumptions demonstrated that one of the lessons history teaches is that history often teaches the wrong lessons: since the East India Company had come to trade and stayed on to rule, Nehru was instinctively suspicious of every foreign businessman, seeing in every Western briefcase the thin end of a neo-imperial wedge. The Gandhian equation of political nationalism with economic self-sufficiency only served to underscore Nehru's prejudice against capitalism, which (far from being synonymous with freedom) was in his mind equated principally with the slavery of his people. Protectionism was the inevitable result: in Jawaharlal's mindset the essential corollary of political independence was economic independence. That this meant a far slower release from poverty for the Indian people he never understood.

There followed the inaptly named Industries (Development and Regulation) Act of 1951, which entrenched regulation and strangled development, and a series of similarly wrongheaded laws that enshrined what Rajaji called the "license-permit-quota Raj." The road to disaster was, as usual, paved with good, even noble, intentions. In December 1954 the government, under Jawaharlal's prodding, formally adopted the goal of "a socialistic pattern of society," and the Congress resolved at Avadi the next year to place the state on the "commanding heights" of the national economy. Within a year the Second Five-Year Plan enshrined industrial self-sufficiency as the goal, to be attained by a state-controlled public sector which would dominate the "commanding heights" of the economy. This public sector would be financed by higher income, wealth, and sales taxes on India's citizenry. India would industrialize, Indians would pay for it, and the Indian government would run the show. This approach was formalized in an Industrial Policy Resolution in 1956 that enshrined state capitalism in India while calling it socialism. Nehru placed bureaucrats rather than entrepreneurs upon the commanding heights, stifled initiative and investment, and spent the rest of his rule presiding over a system that sought to regulate stagnation and divide poverty.

Jawaharlal's approach to the economy was in many ways characteristic of the great flaw that afflicted many freedom fighters: the experience of exclusion and prison gave them an excessively theoretical notion of governance, while nationalist passions injected mistrust of foreigners into policy. Public-sector ventures were run like government departments, overstaffed by bureaucrats with no commitment to their products and no understanding of business. Of course, some good came of Nehru's bad economics: above all, the establishment of a norm of peaceful social change, eschewing both the violence from above favored by the Communists and the laissez-faire conservatism of the landed zamindars and commercial interests. Some would point also to the development of India's industrial and intellectual infrastructure — the dams, steel mills, and institutes of technology that are the most visible result of Jawaharlal's leadership of India's economic policy. Yet others could argue both that these could have come through the private sector and that most of India's public-sector industries were so inefficient that the country would actually have been better off without them. (Certainly the most successful steel plant in India was one set up in the private sector by the Tatas — under British rule.)

Jawaharlal bore a great deal of personal responsibility for the follies of planning, since it was not only led and directed by him in pursuit of his own convictions, but was conducted in a manner that discouraged dissent. All too often, opposition to planning was made to seem like opposition to a fundamental national interest and disloyalty to Jawaharlal himself. Under Nehru, socialism (as he practiced it) became a national dogma, to which his successors stayed loyal long after other developing countries, realizing the folly of his ways, had adopted a different path. Rajaji abandoned him to establish the Swatantra (Independence) Party in 1959 explicitly in protest against Nehru's economic policies, but his was the only dissent from what became a national consensus, and the Swatantra, a pro–free enterprise, pro-Western, conservative party, never acquired enough support to mount a serious challenge to Nehruvian dominance.

The fact was that, following Patel's death, Nehru had progressively turned into a leader without equal and without a rival. Having ousted Tandon and taken on the party presidency himself in 1951, Jawaharlal felt confident enough of his power within three years to relinquish it again. An unthreatening veteran, U. N. Dhebar, was chosen to replace him from January 1955, not by a full ballot of the All-India Congress Committee as in the past, but by the Congress Working Committee under Nehru's chairmanship — a throwback to the days when that body simply rubber-stamped the Mahatma's nominee for president. If some thought that Jawaharlal had become the uncrowned king of the Congress, the adjective was soon remedied by a fifty-year-old Tamilian woman who came up to him unbidden (at the very session in which he gave up his presidency) and placed a golden crown on his balding head. (She then turned to the audience and announced that Jawaharlal was a modern Lord Krishna, confusing the symbols of monarchy with those of mythology.) Nehru promptly handed the crown to Dhebar and asked him to sell it off to benefit the party's coffers. But that minor moment of embarrassment epitomized a reality that Jawaharlal implicitly understood and never exploited.

At least not to the hilt. He could have used the adulation of the masses to turn himself into the dictator his own *Modern Review* article had suggested he might become. It was, indeed, the way most nationalist leaders in developing countries had gone. "Every conceivable argument has been available to tempt Mr. Nehru to forego democratic institutions in India," the philosopher Bertrand Russell wrote. "Illiteracy and poverty, disease and ignorance, a great subcontinent to govern, severe differences between Muslim and Hindu, many scores of languages and varied cultures reflecting a tendency toward a breaking up of the Union." Nehru rejected all these arguments.

Instead he went out of his way to demonstrate respect for the institutions of the state, showing due deference to the president as head of state (and even to the vice president, who had little to do but also outranked the prime minister in protocol terms). He treated Parliament as a serious and august body to which he was accountable, and ensured that his officials treated it as more than a forum for launching policy, but one whose demands and questions had to be treated with due deference. He set the example himself, spending hours in Parliament, suffering Prime Minister's Question Time, and responding seriously to queries unworthy of his attention. He wrote regular monthly letters to the chief ministers of the provinces (later states) to share national and international concerns with them and consult them on issues of policy. He was astonishingly accessible to supplicants and complainants alike. As he explained,

> It is perfectly true that I make myself accessible to every disgruntled element in India. That is my consistent practice. In fact, I go out of my way . . . [to be] accessible to everyone, time permitting. I propose to continue this because that is the way I control these people and, if I may say so, to some extent, India.

During the 1952 elections, when enthusiastic crowds shouted, "*Pandit Nehru zindabad*" ("Long live Pandit Nehru"), he would urge them to shout instead, "*Naya Hindustan zindabad*" ("Long live the new India") or simply "*Jai Hind*" ("Victory to India"). When challenged on fundamental issues of policy his instinct was to offer his resignation: this instantly brought his critics around, but it was not the gesture of a Caesar. It revealed him to be both a democrat and a statesman conscious of his own indispensability.

Indispensable he was. In 1956 the cartoonist R. K. Laxman depicted Nehru playing several instruments simultaneously — a tabla with his right hand, a French horn with his left, a sitar propped up against a shoulder and a pair of cymbals at his feet, and even a party tooter in his mouth — as his audience of Congress stalwarts dutifully marked time. The instruments were labeled "financial affairs," "foreign affairs," "domestic affairs," "Congress affairs," and "SRC affairs" (for the States' Reorganization Commission). Laxman titled his cartoon "The show must go on." No one doubted the polyphonic excellence of the virtuoso performer.

World affairs had always been Jawaharlal's favorite subject, and from the days when he drafted resolutions on international affairs for the annual sessions of the Congress, he enjoyed an unchallenged standing in the country as the maker and enunciator of policy. He carried this on into his prime ministership, retaining the External Affairs portfolio for himself. In one analyst's words, "Nehru's policies were India's, and vice-versa." (Indeed, for all practical purposes, India had no foreign policy, but Nehru did: senior Indian diplomats sometimes learned of policy from Nehru's extempore speeches in Parliament.) This also meant that areas in which Jawaharlal was not particularly interested — geographically (Southeast Asia, Latin America, Africa) or substantively (international commerce and trade relations, defense and security policy) — were largely ignored. Diplomats conducted themselves in his image, focusing on policy, pronouncement, and protocol in the assertion of India's nationhood rather than seeing foreign policy as a means of bringing economic and security benefits to the newly independent country. Given Jawaharlal's extraordinary personal stature, no one dared challenge him; a few who did, early on, were given a taste of the prime minister's temper, and learned quickly to acquiesce in whatever Nehru wanted. As a result, Indian foreign policy emerged whole from the head and heart of one man.

Jawaharlal saw foreign policy as an emanation of national values as he understood and articulated them, derived from Hindu precepts and Buddhist ethics. ("There was no cold war," he once said, "in Ashoka's[8] heart.") The repeated articulation of idealism as the basis of policy (going back to Nehru's invocation of "one world" in his September 1946 broadcast as head of the interim government) was matched by an Olympian disdain for "power politics": when the U.S. offered support for an "Indian Monroe Doctrine" in southern Asia in 1953, Nehru turned John Foster Dulles down with scorn. Indian diplomats who have seen the files swear that at about the same time Jawaharlal also declined a U.S. offer to take the permanent seat on the United Nations Security Council then held, with scant credibility, by Taiwan, urging that it be offered to Beijing instead. Nehru took

[8]Ashoka was a pacifist Buddhist monarch of the third century B.C.

pride in his principled approach to world politics. But it was one thing to fulminate against Great Power machinations, another to run a national foreign policy with little regard to the imperatives of power or the need for a country to bargain from a position of strength.

The eighteen-day state visit of Yugoslav leader Tito (Josip Broz) from December 16, 1954 reflected a decisive shift in India's foreign policy toward the doctrine that became known as "nonalignment." Jawaharlal pulled out all the stops for Tito, a Communist who had thumbed his nose at the Soviet Union and preserved his country's independence from both of the blocs then dividing the world. The joint declaration issued by Nehru and Tito on that occasion spelled out what had become known as the "Panch Sheel," or five principles Jawaharlal wished to see followed in world affairs: respect for sovereignty, nonaggression, noninterference in internal affairs, equality, and "peaceful coexistence." To Nehru, who had signed a similar accord with the People's Republic of China earlier that year, this was the only possible recipe for a self-respecting independent nation and the only means to avoid entanglement in the cold war then bedeviling the world. But the Panch Sheel formula, hailed in China and Yugoslavia, was curiously devoid of any reference to other principles he had advocated during his long struggle for freedom: democracy, human rights, and self-determination. Nor was there any explicit correlation between the principles he was affirming and the needs of the Indian people; foreign policy was an end in itself, rather than a means to promote the security and well-being of the citizenry in whose name it was conducted.

Nowhere was this more apparent than in the fact that, under Nehru, the articulation of foreign policy took on the form of an extended, and excessively moralistic, running commentary on world affairs, once again something more understandable in a liberation movement than in a government. Nehru's foreign policy positions were self-justifying emanations of his intellect; to link them to direct benefits to the Indian people was beneath him. (He refused, for instance, to raise the issue of food aid with Truman in 1949, saying he did not travel with a begging-bowl in his hand.) Nor did he draw the link between foreign policy and national security: if Kashmir and the northern borders had to be secured for India, and Western support was indispensable for this, his approach could scarcely have been better calculated to achieve the opposite effect. Indian sanctimony also periodically antagonized would-be friends among smaller states: in 1957, Thailand cancelled a royal visit to New Delhi after Jawaharlal made scathing references to its "Coca-Cola economy," and the Japanese ambassador to the United Nations reported to Tokyo that his attempts to work with India had been rebuffed on the grounds that its policies were not sufficiently independent as to make collaboration worthwhile. Such positions might have satisfied the amour propre of a self-regarding elite, but to others they were both shortsighted and insufferable, and they would not be forgotten when, in years to come, India needed friends among those it had spurned.

The portrayal of Jawaharlal Nehru's view of the world as synonymous with the larger interests of mankind, and of his voice as that of humanity's conscience (a description actually used by Egyptian leader Gamal

Abdel Nasser), did little to promote good bilateral relations with countries that might have been useful to India. The United States, in particular, found his criticism grating, and his first two visits there, in 1949 and 1956, occurring as they did at a time of widespread fear of communism in America, were not politically successful, though Jawaharlal was accorded all the attention due an international superstar. (The U.S. also prompted his most memorable public quip, when he remarked in 1949, "One must never visit America for the first time.") Nehru's sympathy to China, his improving relations with the Soviet Union, and his opposition to the U.S.'s policy of regional alliances modeled on NATO (Pakistan joined both CENTO, the Central Treaty Organization, and SEATO, the Southeast Asia Treaty Organization) made a clash inevitable. It did not help that the U.S. dismissed nonalignment in trenchant terms — neutrality between good and evil, Dulles famously proclaimed, was itself evil — whereas Nehru prized his independence of thought and action above all else. (A probably apocryphal anecdote has Dulles demanding of Nehru, "Are you for us or against us?" Nehru replied: "Yes.")

The story was a little different with the Soviet Union, with which Jawaharlal sought to establish relations as soon as he took over the interim government in 1946. Stalin regarded him (and for that matter Gandhi) with undisguised suspicion as bourgeois democrats and faux revolutionaries, but the Soviets welcomed any sign that India was breaking free of British (and Western) influence. One of independent India's first ambassadors in Moscow was Jawaharlal's sister Nan, the gracious Vijayalakshmi Pandit (later the first woman president of the United Nations General Assembly). Pandit's appointment was seen as an indication of the importance her brother attached to the relationship with the USSR, but she turned out not to be the wisest choice to convince Moscow of India's anti-imperialist bona fides. The elegant Pandit spent so much time in Moscow's Western diplomatic circles as to provoke one commentator to remark that "India's ambassador forgot that Moscow was not the place to promote good relations between India and the USA." Worse, she was indiscreet enough to express her personal anti-communism to American and British diplomats without first checking for bugs, and the Russians, unamused, did not find it worthwhile to grant her an audience with Stalin.

Things began looking up after the dictator's death. The USSR's willingness to enter into barter trade with India (Russian wheat in exchange for Indian jute and cotton), Moscow's support for India over Kashmir (resulting from Soviet concerns about Western strategic designs in the area), and Nehru's frequent criticisms of the West, all helped smooth the way to better relations. Jawaharlal's visit to the USSR in June 1955 was a huge success ("I am leaving a part of my heart," he declared upon his departure), as was its reciprocation by Khrushchev and Bulganin in November. The Russians were happy to oblige Jawaharlal by building the public-sector steel plants he so craved at a time when the West was insisting that such investment would have to come in the private sector. All the same, Jawaharlal kept his independence from the Communists, playing a neutral role on Korea (where India supported the West on the UN resolution and chaired the Repatriation Commission) and Indochina (though India's chairmanship of the International Control Commission was seen by the U.S. as tilted toward the Communists). India's mediation was also crucial in obtaining the release in 1955 of U.S. pilots downed in China, to which Jawaharlal had paid a visit the previous year, meeting Mao for an hour and Chou En-lai for three (the slogan "*Hindi-Chini bhai bhai*" — "Indians and Chinese are brothers" — was reportedly coined by Nehru at this time).

Jawaharlal's independence from the two major political currents dividing the world did give India the rhetorical leadership of the newly independent nations, who saw in nonalignment a strategy for leveraging their material weakness on the world stage. The undoubted skill of Indian diplomats from Nehru on down in developing and articulating their positions meant that, through most of the 1950s, Nehru's India enjoyed an international stature out of proportion to either its military strength or its material means. Jawaharlal bestrode global diplomacy like a colossus, quoted, admired, and feted; he embodied an emerging world that was just finding its voice, and he did so with grace and style. Even that old curmudgeon Churchill called Nehru the "Light of Asia." (A well-worn story, perhaps apocryphal, has Churchill, recalling the years Nehru spent in British prisons, saying, "You must hate us." To which Jawaharlal replied: "I was taught by a great man never to hate — and never to fear.")

Jawaharlal was the principal mover behind the Afro-

Asian Conference at Bandung in 1955; it was upon his insistence that China was invited to attend, over Western objections (and Israel was not, because of Arab ones). Nehru made a seventy-minute speech in Parliament before the meeting about the great importance of the occasion: for him Bandung marked the epochal moment when a world long dominated by imperial powers finally found its own feet. (He also arranged for an aircraft, Air India's *Kashmir Princess*, to ferry Chinese diplomats to Bandung. The plane was blown up in midair by a time bomb allegedly placed in it by Taiwanese saboteurs; Chou En-lai, the intended target, was not on board.) The conference itself was something of an anticlimax, with cold war divisions diluting the final communiqué, and it is remembered chiefly for the impressive emergence of a soft-spoken but steely Chou En-lai as the moderate face of a Chinese government that had been in the shadows until then. Bandung was followed by the meeting of what the world came to see as the nonaligned triumvirate — Nehru, Nasser, and Tito — at Brioni in July 1956, where the seeds of what was to become a formal movement were sown.

Then came Suez — Nasser's nationalization of the canal, followed by Israeli and Anglo-French invasions of Egyptian territory. The crisis brought out the anticolonial fighter in Jawaharlal. He cabled Nasser, declaring the events "a reversal of history which none of us can tolerate." Nehru worked with the U.S. to ensure the withdrawal of the invaders and later contributed Indian troops to the United Nations peacekeeping operation that followed. His stance of firm opposition to Anglo-French imperialism won him, and India, great popularity in the Muslim world. An American diplomat, the former journalist Phillips Talbot, recalled his astonishment a few years later at seeing portraits of Nehru hanging in so many Egyptian homes. A Pakistani poet, Rais Amrohvi, published a verse declaring that Nehru was the kind of infidel Islam would love to embrace. The same year, though, the Soviet Union invaded Hungary to crush a nationalist ruler, and Jawaharlal, the great international moralist, at first remained silent, explaining to Parliament that "the broad facts were not clear to us." He later declared that "in regard to Hungary or Egypt or anywhere else, any kind of suppression by violent elements of the freedom of the people was an outrage on liberty."

The contrast between his responses to Egypt and to Hungary have often been cited in the West as evidence of Nehruvian hypocrisy, of a moralism that stood somewhere to the left of morality. True, Jawaharlal was instinctively biased against any hint of colonialism, and he was slow to see the Soviet domination of Eastern Europe in similar terms. But his prime ministership was replete with instances of intervention against non-Western tyranny. He protested against the writer Boris Pasternak's detention in the Soviet Union; succeeded in obtaining the Yugoslav dissident Milovan Djilas's release from solitary confinement (though he failed to persuade Tito to free Djilas altogether); and spoke up for jailed democrats in Nepal even at the cost of relations with that vital neighbor's monarch. Despite a foreign policy that many saw as tilted against the West (a part of the world he associated more with imperialism than with freedom), Nehru remained a friend to liberty everywhere.

On the whole, India's international standing in the 1950s was Nehru's principal vindication. The thoughtful Lebanese diplomat Charles Malik, president of the United Nations General Assembly in 1958, paid tribute to five elements of Nehru's leadership of India that bear quoting here: "the adoption and cultivation of representative government through free and democratic institutions; the serious and responsible grappling with the immense social and economic problems of the nation; the retention and cementing of the unity of the Republic through the great leadership that has been displayed; the leading international role that India has played, especially at the United Nations; and the bringing of questions of principle (such as equality, freedom, nondiscrimination, human rights, humanity, peace) to bear upon political questions." The force of example, the nobility of aspiration, and the articulation of India's interests as those of a humanistic universalism, all served to give Nehru's India stature and prestige. India did not speak in terms of nation-state rivalry or patriotic chauvinism; under Nehru it sought an altogether loftier place on the world stage. For all its flaws, this credibility was not easily achieved. In the early years of freedom, for instance, the Soviets scoffed at the idea that India was genuinely independent. Nehru's statements and actions dispelled their skepticism.

Jawaharlal's first decade in office as prime minister of India was crowned by the award to him in 1955 by President Rajendra Prasad of the nation's highest civilian honor, the Bharat Ratna. The "Light of Asia" was now officially the "Jewel of India." There is a photograph of him at the ceremony, in his white *achkan* (formal long coat) with a red rose in the buttonhole, almost boyishly slim, smiling bashfully as the president and an aide-de-camp pin the decoration on him. He was sixty-six and in his pomp, a colossus on the national and international stages.

That first decade of power ended on a dramatic note of triumph. His dominance of the country was once again confirmed in the general elections of 1957, when the Congress Party was returned to office in an overwhelming victory — and with an increased majority in Parliament: 75 percent of the seats in the House and 65 percent in the state legislatures.

There was almost nowhere left to go but down.

9

"Free Myself from this Daily Burden": 1957–1964

On April 29, 1958, Jawaharlal Nehru announced his wish to resign. He did so in a public statement to the Congress parliamentary party, in which he pleaded fatigue and staleness. "The work of a prime minister," he said, "allows no respite, it is continuous and unceasing. . . . There is little time for quiet thinking. I feel now that I must . . . free myself from this daily burden and think of myself as an individual citizen of India and not as prime minister." He was not quite halfway between sixty-eight and sixty-nine; he had been head of the government for almost a dozen of those years, but he was as fit and vigorous as many half his age, practicing yoga daily and working late into the night. Had his offer been accepted, it would have set a democratic precedent around the developing world, none of whose first independence leaders had ever resigned voluntarily, nor would until the 1970s. The Congress parliamentary party, though, refused to entertain the thought; taken aback by the statement, they held an emergency meeting to urge Nehru to stay on. Both Eisenhower and Khrushchev wrote expressing their hope that Jawaharlal would not leave. In the end, he settled for a long holiday in his beloved mountains instead, where he climbed with all the ardor of his youth until stopped by his doctors at 13,600 feet.

His daughter, Indira, accompanied him on the holiday. Through the 1950s she had been his official hostess and constant companion, to the detriment of her marriage. When she moved into the prime ministerial residence, Teen Murti House, to assume a full-time role by her father's side, her husband stayed away. Feroze Gandhi was a Congress member of Parliament, with something of a reputation for brashly taking on his own party's government. But he was loudly resentful of his wife's decision to support her father rather than her husband, and though the two never formally separated, their marriage was reduced to a shell, their old love desiccated into ritual. In 1958 Feroze suffered a stroke, and in September 1960 he died of a heart attack. Indira became physically ill upon hearing the news. But if Jawaharlal ever reproached himself for having deprived his daughter of the consolations of a normal married life — something he himself had hardly enjoyed — he never made it known.

Some critics, mostly with the benefit of hindsight, have suggested that Nehru was grooming his daughter to succeed him. There is no evidence whatsoever that such a thought crossed his mind. Of course, being his official hostess provided Indira with a unique political education at close quarters, and she soon revealed a taste for affairs of state, both domestic and international. But Jawaharlal took no steps to promote her as a possible successor; he did not appoint her to his cabinet, despite public calls from partymen for him to do so, and she rates as an also-ran in Welles Hangen's famous speculative 1963 book, *After Nehru, Who?* The worst that can be said is that Nehru did not object when others in the Congress Party pushed his daughter into politics, at first as organizer of the party's women's wing in 1953 and most notably when they elected her president of the Congress Party nationally for 1959. She proved a fierce and partisan official, leading the Congress into the streets against the elected Communist government in the state of Kerala and pressuring the government of India to dismiss the state authorities for failing to maintain law and order. But she did not seek (and Jawaharlal did not encourage) reelection.

Nehru, ever the democrat, confronted the issue of succession directly in a 1961 interview: "I am not trying to start a dynasty. I am not capable of ruling from the grave. How terrible it would be if I, after all I have said about the processes of democratic government, were to attempt to handpick a successor. The best I can do for India is to help our people as a whole to generate new leadership as it may be needed." But by 1961, despite visible exhaustion, he had given up all thought of retirement. When Norman Cousins asked him about it, Nehru "looked as though nothing would be more unwelcome. . . . More than ever, we realized that Nehru loved his job and had no thought of leaving it." Sadly, he had done little to encourage and groom credible alternative leadership.

But it was never easy to imagine an alternative. Jawaharlal was a man of seemingly inexhaustible energy who put in sixteen- or seventeen-hour workdays throughout his life. Punctual and courteous to a fault, a man of regular habits, sustained by a simple diet and daily yogic exercise, he always demanded more of himself than of others. His first Principal Private Secretary, H. V. R. Iengar, recounted how, after an exhausting and dispiriting day touring riot-racked Punjab in August 1947,

> round about midnight, we all dispersed, with another program, equally heavy and tragic, to start at six the next morning. I went to bed exhausted, both physically and in spirit. When, with some difficulty, I got ready early that morning to go to the airport, the P.A. [personal assistant] showed me a pile of letters, telegrams and memoranda which the prime minister had dictated after everybody had dispersed. The P.M. had gone to bed at 2 A.M. but was ready at 5:30 to start another day.

Iengar saw this punishing pace as "a case of the utter triumph of the spirit over the body, of a consuming passion for public work overcoming the normal mechanics of the human frame."

The negative side of this capacity lay in Nehru's obsession with detail — not merely in spending his time on matters unworthy of the attention of a head of government, but on trivialities like a painting improperly hung

on a wall, or an untidy room, which would upset him to the point that he could not work if it was not redressed. As prime minister and external affairs minister he obsessed about the details of his files as few other ministers did. "Panditji liked to do much of his civil servants' work for them," one diplomat recalled ruefully. "I suppose it gave him vicarious satisfaction to beat them at their own game — noting, drafting, replying to every kind of letter. . . . His love for the quick disposal of paper also inevitably led to dispensing with a basic rule of the civil servant, the requirement of consulting previous papers on the subject." Added to this was a tendency to enjoy conversation for its own sake, oblivious to the far greater priorities demanding the prime minister's attention. One British official assigned to the Defense Ministry in the late 1950s noted that Jawaharlal "liked chatting about the world in general. . . . When I was with him, he just chatted. It was curious. I was surprised. He chatted."

The roots of this may have lain in Jawaharlal's youth. The domineering Motilal adored and spoiled his son, but may well have instilled in him a tragic flaw for a leader — an instinctive sense that the ultimate responsibility for decision lay elsewhere than in himself. Knowing that his father, and later the Mahatma, were there encouraged in Jawaharlal a tendency to temporize and vacillate, to indulge in reflection and thinking aloud, and yet not commit to a concrete decision. During the nationalist struggle Subhas Bose bitterly reproached Jawaharlal for this. In the later years of his rule this tendency had unfortunate consequences. His close friend Syed Mahmud suggested that Jawaharlal was "not temperamentally made for pursuing decisions to their ultimate execution at the lowest levels."

Indira and Jawaharlal presided over an unusual household for a busy prime minister. The official residence overflowed with animals — dogs of assorted breeds (including not a few mongrels), a pair of Himalayan pandas, peacocks and parrots, squirrels and deer, and (until they became too large to keep safely at home) three tiger cubs. Indira's two sons, Rajiv and Sanjay, had the run of the place (sometimes literally on their grandfather's back). Teen Murti was also constantly full of house guests, including, once a year, Edwina Mountbatten. Friends would drop in for dinner, where the table manners of Cambridge were applied to the cuisine of Allahabad. The gardens of Teen Murti were full every morning with ordinary people who came for an "open house," where they could petition, talk with, or simply receive a "darshan" (a regal sight) of their prime minister.

Jawaharlal's personality was mercurial. He could be utterly charming to total strangers, witty, engaging, and even (in the right mood) frivolous: there are accounts of his dinnertime impersonations of world leaders that had his guests in splits, and he would often oblige casual dinner guests to don one of the foreign national costumes he had been presented with on his travels. Many foreigners who met him in the 1930s and well into the 1950s speak of a captivating figure, with great intellectual breadth, blessed with intelligence and curiosity as well as impeccable manners, who disarmed his interlocutors with his warmth, wit, courtesy, and grace. (Phillips Talbot, who first met him as a visiting student in 1939 and over the next twenty-five years as journalist, scholar, and diplomat, declared more than six decades after that first encounter: "I still find it difficult to be objective about Nehru. He was enormously captivating, warm, intelligent, brilliant; inspiring even when angry.") The actor and filmmaker Charlie Chaplin recounted in his autobiography a marvelous story of Nehru in 1953 chattering away animatedly to the movie legend in the back of his car while his driver, to Chaplin's consternation, careened through Swiss mountain roads at a death-defying seventy miles per hour.

Nehru's close friend Syed Mahmud was immediately struck, upon first meeting Jawaharlal, by his manners, which were those of "an upper-class English gentleman"; but his level of courtesy and consideration was extravagantly Indian. When Mahmud explained his reliance on a traveling servant by saying how much he hated folding and spreading his bedding on the bunk of the train, Jawaharlal took on the chore himself, and continued to make and unmake Mahmud's bed whenever the two traveled together over a period of decades. The Ghanaian leader Kwame Nkrumah told the story of how, on a winter visit to India, he was about to leave by train for the cold north when

> Nehru unexpectedly arrived at the station looking rather extraordinary in an oversized overcoat. . . . "I know it is too big for me, but I think it should be just right for you. . . . Try it on." I tried it on and it was, as he had said, just right. I put my hands proudly in the pockets and discovered fresh surprises. In

> one there was a warm wool scarf and in the other a pair of warm gloves.

This courtesy was not only for VIPs: discovering on a visit to Kashmir that his stenographer's suitcase had been mislaid and that the poor man was shivering in a thin cotton shirt, the prime minister personally ensured that a sweater and jacket were provided to him. Jawaharlal never forgot a sibling's birthday, even when in prison. He was also so good with children (who knew him as "Chacha," or Uncle Nehru) that his birthday began to be celebrated across India, even while he was alive, as Children's Day.

Yet the same Jawaharlal could also be imperious and short-tempered. He would often lash out publicly at some unfortunate official who was in no position to defend himself. The Ceylonese leader Solomon Bandaranaike described him as "a delicately nurtured aristocrat with high-strung nerves. . . . He often uses up his nervous energy and that makes him sometimes short-tempered and irritable." Bandaranaike recounted with wry amusement lunching with Nehru as an admiring crowd gathered and Jawaharlal erupted, "I just cannot eat in public." The crowd was dispersed and Bandaranaike mused, "There speaks the sensitive aristocrat." Nehru was also capable of behaving in a manner so remote and brooding that he seemed to be thinking of anyone but his interlocutor, and (particularly in his later years) retreating into lengthy and impenetrable silences even when receiving visitors. He was not just moody; many felt a barrier existed between him and even those closest to him. He was often described as the loneliest man in India.

Despite (or perhaps because of) these paradoxical qualities, Jawaharlal enjoyed the attentions of several distinguished women, many of whom, at least if Stanley Wolpert's speculations are to be believed, may have become his lovers. Through much of the 1950s Edwina Mountbatten and Jawaharlal exchanged annual visits; the French author Catherine Clément has spun an elaborate romance out of these twice-yearly encounters (Edwina staying with him at Teen Murti, Jawaharlal with her at the Mountbatten estate in England, Broadlands). Others suggest that though the opportunity certainly existed, and the two exchanged intimate letters testifying to the intensity of their friendship, there is no proof the relationship was ever consummated. In 1960 Edwina died in Borneo with letters from Jawaharlal scattered about her bed. He was an ardent and prolific correspondent to a number of women: his letters to Padmaja Naidu, Sarojini's daughter and herself a frequent overnight guest at his house, are perhaps among the most exquisite love letters ever written by an Indian public figure. But the speculation is largely irrelevant: Jawaharlal's major aphrodisiac, as Talbot put it, was clearly politics.

Perhaps the most interesting description of Nehru at this time (when he had, so to speak, just crested the peak of his success but not yet begun to sense his own decline) comes from the account of another who combined the burdens of governmental office with the acuity of the writer-philosopher, the Frenchman André Malraux, who called on Jawaharlal in 1958. Nehru had "a Roman face with a slight heaviness about the lower lip which gave his apparently 'posed' smile the seductiveness which a suggestion of innocence imparts to a great man," wrote Malraux. Nehru's voice and bearing revealed "beneath the patrician intellectual the English gentleman's ease and self-possession which he had doubtless learned to emulate in his youth. . . . His hand gestures, once so expansive, were now turned inward toward his body, the fingers almost closed. And . . . these chilly gestures . . . gave his authority a charm such as I have never since encountered." Malraux noted delightfully that Nehru "meant what he said, like the few great statesmen I have met, and like most of the painters."

Critics have painted an unedifying picture of a Jawaharlal increasingly out of touch with reality in his last years in office, prone to public expressions of self-doubt, drifting into decisions delayed by his own tendency to see both sides of every question, an intellectual dreamer who gave expression to ideas but not to their implementation. Though much of that is true, it paints a simplistic picture. There were both triumphs and setbacks in his life and work, many challenges successfully surmounted and one crushing defeat.

Domestic issues continued to press in upon him — a Naga tribal insurgency in the northeast, Master Tara Singh's demands for a Sikh-majority state in the Punjab, anti-Hindi agitation in Madras (where the avowedly secessionist Dravida Munnetra Kazhagam Party was gaining ground in its attacks on north Indian domination). Nehru dealt with these through a combination of shrewdness (postponing the proposed adoption of Hindi as the official national language until 1965), democracy (insisting that the Sikhs could flourish in free India without needing a Sikh-majority state, while backing a tough Sikh Congressman, Pratap Singh Kairon, as chief minister of Punjab), and repression (turning the army on the Nagas). All three came into play over Kashmir, where he explored every hope of a settlement, only to be thwarted each time. Just before his death he released Sheikh Abdullah from jail and sent him to Pakistan to negotiate a new accommodation. (It was at a press conference in Muzaffarabad that the Sheikh learned the news of Jawaharlal's passing; he wept openly at the loss of his former comrade-in-arms, who had sadly become his jailer.)

Jawaharlal — the man who had in his younger days been known to leap off the stage and physically attack hecklers in his audience — became an Olympian presence at public meetings around the country. Nehru made magnificent speeches, usually without notes, but he was not a great orator. The British statesman Lord Pethick-Lawrence described Jawaharlal's style as prime minister:

> Unlike a European or American orator he does not commence on a bold or emphatic note or end with a carefully prepared rhetorical peroration. His voice begins quietly; almost imperceptibly, like a piece of Indian music, it rises to a height of passionate pleading and fades away at the end into silence. And his listeners are greatly moved alike by his sincerity and his restraint.

Sometimes they were not; even an admirer, the industrialist S. P. Jain, conceded that "occasionally his speeches are rambling, sometimes trite, sometimes reflective and unrelated to the immediate subject of the debate." But "it is the personality of the man rather than his oratory that holds attention." And through the strength of his personality Jawaharlal held the country together and nurtured its democracy. But his sense of mass public opinion became increasingly suspect: as one historian put it, "Nehru addressed the Indian masses as a democrat, but the Indian masses revered him as a demigod. . . . In his last years he had no means of feeling the pulse of the people he wanted to serve. The masses were either mute or would throw him their acclaim at crowded meetings."

Nor could Jawaharlal prevent the growth of the corruption which his own statist policies facilitated. The image of the self-sacrificing Congressmen in homespun gave way to that of the professional politicians the educated middle classes came to despise, sanctimonious windbags clad hypocritically in khadi who spouted socialist rhetoric while amassing uncountable (and unaccountable) riches by manipulating governmental favors. With licenses and quotas for every business activity, petty politicians grew rich by profiting from the power to permit. In 1959, in a birthday tribute, no less, Jawaharlal's sister Krishna (Betty) wrote sadly: "Nehru the Prime Minister no longer remembers or adheres to the ideals or dreams that Jawahar the Rebel had. . . . [H]e can no longer arouse his people as he did in years gone by, for he has allowed himself to be surrounded by those who are known to be opportunists and the entire Government machinery, corrupt and heavy with intrigue, rules the land with no hope of an honest hearing from any quarter." A sympathetic biographer, Frank Moraes, wrote that "in India today there is no one to restrain or guide Nehru. He is Caesar, and from Caesar one can appeal only to Caesar."

The stench of corruption reached Jawaharlal's own circles three times in the later years of his rule: when his finance minister, T. T. Krishnamachari, was obliged to resign in 1958 over improprieties in a life insurance scandal (it was Feroze Gandhi's muckraking that brought about Krishnamachari's downfall); when his friend Jayanti Dharma Teja, whom Nehru had helped set up a major shipping line, defaulted on loans and skipped the country; and when Jawaharlal's own private secretary since 1946, M. O. Mathai, who was accused both of spying for the CIA and of accumulating an ill-gotten fortune, was forced to resign in 1959. In none of these cases was there the slightest suggestion that Jawaharlal had profited personally in any way from the actions of his associates, but they again confirmed that Nehru's loyalty exceeded his judgment. (And in dozens of other cases where corruption was not an issue, he picked unsuitable aides and persisted in his support for them well after their ineptitude had been revealed.) By the late 1950s he was widely considered a poor judge of men, and not merely by his critics. An admirer and former cabinet colleague, Rajkumari Amrit Kaur, put it bluntly:

> He is not a good judge of character and is therefore easily deceived. He is not averse to flattery and there is a conceit in him which makes him at once intolerant of criticism and may even warp his better

> judgment. His very loyalty to friends blinds him to their faults. For this very reason he is not ruthless enough as a leader and his leadership is weakened thereby.

But Nehru's own conduct was exemplary; when in 1957 the city of Allahabad levied a trivial wealth tax on his property there, Nehru insisted it be assessed five times higher.

The task of nation-building remained a vital preoccupation for Jawaharlal. India's freedom from colonial rule was not complete with the adoption of the republican Constitution on January 26, 1950. France and Portugal still maintained territories on Indian soil. The French negotiated an amicable withdrawal from their *comptoirs* in 1954, but the Portuguese, under the Salazar dictatorship, insisted their territory of Goa was a full-fledged province of Portugal, and enjoyed the overt support of Britain and the United States for their claim. The international dimension prompted Jawaharlal not to opt for the "police action" that had overrun Hyderabad and Junagadh, but domestic outrage over the continuation of the foreign enclave spilled over into the colony as nonviolent satyagrahis crossed the border in protest and were shot by Portuguese border guards. After more than a decade of vacillation, during which he agonized over Gandhi's injunctions not to use force even in the pursuit of just ends, Nehru ordered the Army to move at the end of 1961. Goa fell within twenty-six hours; the hopelessly outgunned Portuguese governor surrendered without a fight. India weathered international opprobrium easily enough, though President Kennedy tartly suggested to the Indian ambassador in Washington that India might now consider delivering fewer self-righteous sermons on nonviolence. The victory in Goa gave Jawaharlal a great surge of domestic popularity, which helped carry him and the Congress to another resounding victory in the general elections of 1962. It would be his last.

His final visit to the United States occurred in November 1961, during the presidency of a man who had long admired him, John F. Kennedy. But Nehru was at his worst, moody and sullen at times, didactic and superior at others. The two statesmen failed to hit it off; JFK was later quoted as saying this was the worst state visit he had suffered. Nehru no longer attracted uncritical admiration. His positions, both domestic and international, were seen by many as hypocritical. A satirical view of Nehru's inconsistencies came in the words of the American poet Ogden Nash, who published a savage piece of doggerel, "The Pandit":

> Just how shall we define a Pandit?
> It's not a panda, nor a bandit.
> But rather a Pandora's box
> Of sophistry and paradox.
> Though Oxford [*sic*] gave it a degree
> It maintains its neutrality
> By quietly hating General Clive
> As hard as if he were alive.
> On weighty international questions
> It's far more Christian than most Christians;
> It's ever eager, being meek
> To turn someone else's cheek.
> Oft has it said all men are brothers,

And set that standard up for others,
Yet as it spoke it gerrymandered
Proclaiming its private Pakistandard.
The neutral pandit walks alone,
And if abroad, it casts a stone,
It walks impartial to the last,
Ready at home to stone a caste.
Abandon I for now the pandit,
I fear I do not understand it.

A few months before Goa, in September 1961, Nehru, Nasser, and Tito had met in Belgrade to complete the task they had begun in Brioni five years earlier — the formal creation of the Nonaligned movement. The occasion saw the passage of various resolutions condemning war and calling for nuclear disarmament, of which Nehru was inordinately proud. It was a telling indication of the gulf between his view of the world and the international realities with which he had to deal.

It is sometimes true that one's greatest failures emerge from one's greatest passions. Foreign policy was Jawaharlal Nehru's favorite subject, his area of unchallenged expertise. China had been a source of intense fascination since his youth, a country he frequently sought to visit and for whose leaders he had expressed great admiration ever since his speech at the Anti-Imperialist Congress in Brussels in 1927. Yet it was his failure to manage India's relationship with China that, more than anything else, blighted his last years of office and contributed to his final decline.

After signing the Panch Sheel agreement with China

in 1954 and helping Chou En-lai emerge into the limelight in Bandung in 1955, Jawaharlal embarked on a starry-eyed phase of "*Hindi-Chini bhai-bhai*" which seemed willfully blind to the real divergence of interests between the two countries at that time. Bandung marked the beginning of Sino-Pakistani contacts that would soon flower into a vital alliance, for Beijing was more conscious of its geopolitical place in the world than Nehru's New Delhi was. China's reestablishment of its authority over Tibet in 1950 brought the People's Liberation Army to the frontiers of India along a British-demarcated boundary (the McMahon Line) that Beijing had never recognized. This should have prompted a certain amount of realism about national security in New Delhi; but Nehru, anxious to avoid any rupture of the anticolonial solidarity he felt with China, resisted Patel's demands that India set out a clear (and by implication assertive) position on the border issue. His policy instead became an uneasy amalgam of idealist rhetoric about Sino-Indian relations on the one hand and firm assurances to Parliament that India would hold its border at the McMahon Line. Nehru did not, however, press Beijing to come to a negotiated agreement on the border, preferring to take at face value a statement by Chou in 1952 that China had no border dispute with India. In April 1954 Nehru formally recognized Tibet as a full-fledged part of China, giving up assorted British-era rights India had acquired there, without seizing the opportunity to obtain a border agreement in return.

Through the mid-1950s, and particularly after Bandung, Jawaharlal seemed to see himself as virtually a patron of China, a position hardly likely to be well received in Beijing. Jawaharlal saw it as India's duty to sponsor China's arrival on the world scene and to lead the demand for Beijing to assume its rightful place at the United Nations. An escalating series of disputes and mutual protests over territorial issues were treated in New Delhi as minor misunderstandings that should not be allowed to cloud the larger picture. So self-delusion compounded arrogance. Nehru was also impervious to China's increasing irritation with what its leaders saw as Indian pretensions to Great Power standing globally and specifically in Asia, a position which by size and strength Beijing viewed as more naturally China's. By 1959 Beijing openly declared that the Sino-Indian boundary had never been formally delineated and that China had never recognized the McMahon Line drawn by British imperialists. When China cracked down on a Tibetan rebellion that year, New Delhi's grant of asylum to the fleeing Dalai Lama and thousands of his followers in March 1959 further embittered relations.

But by that point Nehru had given away all of India's cards. When the shooting started with a series of border incidents later that year, India was found woefully unprepared. Yet Nehru refused to believe China would ever embark on war with India, and did unconscionably little to prepare his forces for one. His defense minister from 1957 on was the leftist ideologue Krishna Menon, a votary of self-reliance who refused to import defense equipment and turned the military factories into production lines for hairpins and pressure-cookers. In 1959 Menon clashed publicly with the army chief, General

Thimayya, who had to be persuaded by Nehru to withdraw his resignation after being denounced as pro-West by his own minister. In the next couple of years the warnings from the armed forces about their inability to protect Indian positions without additional resources proliferated, but were largely ignored by Nehru and Menon. As late as August 1961 Jawaharlal told Parliament that India did not believe in war, and would not act "in a huff" but behave with "wisdom and strength," complacent banalities that revealed neither wisdom nor strength. In November that year, on the basis of a flawed intelligence estimate from another trusted acolyte, the head of the Intelligence Bureau, B. N. Mullick, Nehru instructed the army "to patrol as far forward as possible from our present positions . . . without getting involved in a clash with the Chinese." But the patrols moved without adequate logistical support, and the troops were at their most vulnerable just as clashes became inevitable. On September 8, 1962, the Chinese crossed the McMahon Line, claiming self-defense against Indian "aggression," then stopped. Nehru and Menon persuaded themselves that the incident was only a skirmish, and each traveled on planned visits abroad. But neither seemed to have realized the extent of the Chinese mobilization. On October 20 waves of Chinese troops poured across the border. Full-fledged war had broken out.

It was a rout. The war lasted a month, with only ten days of actual fighting; brave Indian troops, underequipped and understrength, without firewood or adequate tentage, many wearing canvas shoes in the Himalayan snows, and short of ammunition for their antiquated Lee Enfield rifles, were simply overwhelmed. On November 21 China, with its forces seemingly unstoppable, unilaterally declared a cease-fire and then withdrew from much of the territory it had captured, retaining some 2,500 square miles in the western sector. It had, in the words of Liu Shao-chi, taught India a lesson. Nehru's grand international pretensions had been cut down to size.

A calamitous military defeat was only the most evident of Nehru's setbacks. His foreign policy lay in a shambles, as the Soviet Union and most of the nonaligned world remained neutral in the conflict and India turned to the United States (itself in the midst of the Cuban Missile Crisis) for help — including, to the astonishment of Jawaharlal's ambassador in Washington, his cousin B. K. Nehru, American military aircraft. Nehru's stature as the leader of the newly liberated colonial peoples and his authority to speak for the "Third World" had been dealt a major blow. But this time Jawaharlal did not offer to resign. The public and Parliament turned on Menon instead; not even the loyal support of Nehru could save him, and on November 7 Menon was forced out of the government. Nehru, let down by those in whom he had placed such trust, betrayed by his own idealism, was a broken man. In April 1963 he suffered the first of a series of serious illnesses that would mark his rapid downward spiral toward death.

And yet one should not overlook the transcendent irony of 1962, the reawakening of an Indian nationalism that Jawaharlal had once incarnated but had since sought to subsume in idealist internationalism. For the first time since that midnight moment of independence, the country rallied together as one: housewives knit sweaters for the soldiers on the Himalayan front and donated their gold jewelry to the servicemen's fund, moviegoers stood respectfully to attention as the national anthem played in theaters after the film, schoolchildren discovered a sense of patriotism that had nothing to do with overthrowing the English. In the moment of his greatest failure, the preeminent voice of Indian freedom unwittingly gave a new boost to a nationalist resurgence. War, and defeat, destroyed illusions but nurtured resolve, tightening the bonds Nehru had helped put in place to hold his disparate country together.

The eighteen months left to him after the Chinese debacle added little to Jawaharlal Nehru's reputation. In August 1963, forty opposition members of Parliament sponsored a no-confidence motion against his government. The Congress's crushing majority meant that it was easily defeated, but a new slogan was heard in the House: "Quit, Nehru, quit!" Three months later, in November 1963, Jawaharlal launched India's own space program, a moment immortalized in a photograph by Henri Cartier-Bresson showing a rocket part being carried on the back of a bicycle. Six years earlier Jawaharlal had inaugurated India's first atomic research reactor. Nuclear power and space technology: there was no limit to his scientific aspirations for India, and yet the country was moored in the bicycle age at least partly because of his unwillingness to open up its economy to the world.

By 1964 the signs of mortality were impossible to ignore. Jawaharlal was visibly ailing; the puffy face, the sunken eyes, the shuffling gait were of a man in irreversible decline. His visits to Parliament were, in the words of a senior opposition member, those of "an old man, looking frail and fatigued . . . with a marked stoop in his gait . . . [and] slow, faltering steps, clutching the backrests of benches for support as he descended." Nehru suffered a cerebral stroke at the annual Congress session in January and missed most of it, but within days was back in New Delhi trying to manage his usual routine. Work was his lifeblood. "If I lie down in bed for even a week," he declared, "I know I will not get up!" That moment was not long in arriving. A second stroke felled him on May 17, but he resumed his schedule within days. On May 22 he told a press conference, in response to a question about whether he should not settle the question of his successor in his own lifetime: "My life is not coming to an end so soon." On May 27, 1964 — a date astonishingly foretold five years earlier by one of his ministers' favorite astrologers, Haveli Ram Joshi — Jawaharlal Nehru passed away in his sleep after a massive aortic rupture. On his bedside table were found, jotted down in his own hand, the immortal lines from Robert Frost's "Stopping by Woods on a Snowy Evening":

> The woods are lovely, dark and deep,
> But I have promises to keep,
> And miles to go before I sleep.
> And miles to go before I sleep.

Sleep had come to Nehru at the age of seventy-four. The nation was plunged into mourning; tributes poured in from around the world. An earthquake rocked the capital on the day of his death, a portentous omen to some. Cynics waited for the survivors to fight over the spoils; many predicted India's inevitable disintegration. But Jawaharlal had prepared his people well, instilling in them the habits of democracy, a respect for parliamentary procedure, and faith in the constitutional system. There were no succession squabbles. Lal Bahadur Shastri, a modest figure of unimpeachable integrity and considerable political and administrative acumen, was elected India's second prime minister. The country wept, and moved on.

Years earlier Jawaharlal had repeated a question posed to him by an American interviewer: "My legacy to India? Hopefully, it is 400 million people capable of governing themselves." The numbers had grown, but in the peaceful transfer of power that followed his death, Jawaharlal Nehru had left his most important legacy.

His last will and testament, written in 1954 when he was not yet sixty-five, was released to the nation upon his death. In it he spoke of his gratitude for the love and affection of the Indian people and his hope that he would not prove unworthy of them. He asked that his body be cremated and the ashes transported to Allahabad, his birthplace, where a "small handful" was to be "thrown in the Ganga." This last request would not have been surprising from a devout man, but from India's most famous agnostic, a man who openly despised temples and was never known to have worshipped at any Hindu shrine in his long life, it came as a surprise. Nehru's reasons, spelled out in his will, had little to do with religion:

> The Ganga, especially, is the river of India, beloved of her people, round which are intertwined her

> racial memories, her hopes and fears, her songs of triumph, her victories and her defeats. She has been a symbol of India's age-long culture and civilization, ever-changing, ever-flowing, and yet ever the same Ganga. She reminds me of the snow-covered peaks and the deep valleys of the Himalayas, which I have loved so much, and of the rich and vast plains below, where my life and work have been cast. Smiling and dancing in the morning sunlight, and dark and gloomy and full of mystery as the evening shadows fall, a narrow, slow and graceful stream in winter and a vast, roaring thing during the monsoon, broad-bosomed almost as the sea, and with something of the sea's power to destroy, the Ganga has been to me a symbol and a memory of the past of India, running into the present, and flowing on to the great ocean of the future. And though I have discarded much of past tradition and custom, and am anxious that India should rid herself of all shackles that bind and constrain her and divide her people, . . . I do not wish to cut myself off from the past completely. I am proud of that great inheritance that has been, and is, ours, and I am conscious that I too, like all of us, am a link in that unbroken chain which goes back to the dawn of history in the immemorial past of India.

This was Jawaharlal at his finest: lyrical, sentimental, passionately combining a reverence for the past with his aspirations for the future, making the most sacred river of Hinduism into a force for cultural unity, a torrent that unites history with hope. There is nothing in Nehru's use of the Ganga as symbol that could alienate an Indian Muslim or Christian. Here was the magic of Indian nationalism as no one else could express it, capped by a concluding request:

> The major portion of my ashes should . . . be carried high up into the air in an airplane and scattered from that height over the fields where the peasants of India toil, so that they might mingle with the dust and soil . . . and become an indistinguishable part of India.

During his years as prime minister, many at home and abroad could not distinguish Jawaharlal Nehru from the country he so unchallengeably led. That task would now become literally impossible. In death, as in life, Jawaharlal would become India.

10

"India Must Struggle against Herself": 1889–1964–2003

"My presents," Jawaharlal Nehru wrote to his daughter Indira from prison on her thirteenth birthday in November 1930, "cannot be very material or solid. They can only be of the air and of the mind and of the spirit, such as a good fairy might have bestowed on you — things that even the high walls of prison cannot stop." These gifts he bestowed in plenty, and when he died in 1964, Nehru's legacy to the nation and the world seemed secure. A towering figure in national politics and on the international stage, the reflective, mercurial Nehru had — in innumerable books and speeches, but also in his conduct as a prime minister — developed and articulated a worldview that embodied the aspirations of his generation, of his country, and (many believed) of the developing postcolonial world as a whole. "We are all Nehruvians," a senior Indian official told me years later, with conviction and pride, of his colleagues in the Indian ruling establishment.

Two and a half decades after that remark, there are fewer Nehruvians in office. Indeed, Nehruvianism seems to have lost both power and allure. Nehru is criticized, even derided, by votaries of an alternative version of Indian nationalism, one that claims to be more deeply rooted in the land (and therefore in its religious traditions and customary prejudices). His mistakes are magnified, his achievements belittled. How are we, today, to parse his legacy? Nehru's impact on India rested on four major pillars — democratic institution-building, staunch pan-Indian secularism, socialist economics at home, and a foreign policy of nonalignment. All four remain as official tenets of Indian governance, but all have been challenged, and strained to the breaking point, by the developments of recent years.

"The world's largest democracy" remains the sobriquet of which all Indians are proud. India became that under the tutelage of a man so unquestionably its leader — so unchallengeably the personification of its very freedom — that all he needed to do if anyone opposed him was to threaten to resign. Nehru usually got his way. And yet he was a convinced democrat, a man so wary of the risks of autocracy that, at the crest of his rise, he authored an anonymous article warning Indians of the dangers of giving dictatorial temptations to Jawaharlal Nehru. As prime minister he carefully nurtured democratic institutions, paying careful deference to the country's ceremonial presidency, regularly writing letters to the chief ministers of India's states explaining his policies, subjecting himself to cross-examination in Parliament by a fractious opposition, taking care not to interfere with the judiciary (on the one occasion where he publicly criticized a judge, he apologized the next day to the individual and to the chief justice of India). Though he was, in the celebrated Indian metaphor, the immense banyan tree in whose shade no other plant could grow, he made sure that every possible flora flourished in the forest.

In his 1937 *Modern Review* article in which he had anonymously portrayed himself as a potential dictator "sweeping aside the paraphernalia of a slow-moving democracy," Jawaharlal had added the revealing aside: "He is far too much of an aristocrat for the crudity and vulgarity of fascism." As an aristocrat he disdained autocracy, and this paradox illuminated his nurturing of Indian democracy. If there was something tutelary about it — the idol of the masses dispensing democracy like so much *prasad*[9] to the worshipping throngs — that was a necessary phase in the process of educating a largely illiterate, overwhelmingly poor people in the rights and prerogatives that came with freedom. There is no doubt that Nehru romanticized his connection to the Indian masses. As he wrote to Edwina in 1951: "Wherever I have been, vast multitudes gather at my meetings and I love to compare them, their faces, their dresses, their reactions to me and what I say. . . . I try to probe into the minds and

[9] *Prasad,* literally a blessing, is food offered to an idol in a temple ritual and then distributed to the worshippers.

hearts of these multitudes. . . . The effort to explain in simple language our problems and our difficulties, and to reach the minds of these simple folk is both exhausting and exhilarating."

When Dr. Rafiq Zakaria began a biographical essay on Nehru for his compilation *A Study of Nehru*, published to mark the prime minister's seventieth birthday, he noted the "extravagance" of the Indian people's love of Jawaharlal:

> They have idolized him; they have worshipped him. Even in the inaccessible tribal areas, his name is a household word; to the illiterate villagers he has become almost a god. To most Indians he has symbolized everything that is good and noble and beautiful in life. Even his faults are admirable; his weaknesses, lovable. In a land of hero-worship he has become the hero of heroes. To criticize him is wrong; to condemn him is blasphemous. . . . They may be dissatisfied with his party; they may be unhappy under his Government, but such is their devotion to the man that he is not blamed for anything.

Yet by his speeches, his exhortations, and above all by his own personal example, Jawaharlal imparted to the institutions and processes of democracy a dignity that placed it above challenge from would-be tyrants. He instituted a public audience at his home every morning where ordinary people could come to petition or talk with their prime minister. His speeches were an extended conversation with the people of India. "Sometimes," wrote the journalist A. M. Rosenthal, "he talked angrily to his India and sometimes he shrieked at it and denounced it and said it was just impossible, impossible. Sometimes he courted his India, laughed with it, and was merry and delicate and understanding. But it was always as if Jawaharlal Nehru was looking into the eyes of India and India was just one soul."

And yet Jawaharlal was often described by his critics as the last Englishman left in India; the British journalist Malcolm Muggeridge called him the last viceroy. By Nehru's own admission as a young man, "I had imbibed most of the prejudices of Harrow and Cambridge and in my likes and dislikes I was perhaps more an Englishman than an Indian. . . . And so I returned to India as much prejudiced in favor of England and the English as it was possible for an Indian to be." The writer Nirad Chaudhuri declared that Nehru was "completely out of touch with the Indian life even of his time, except with the life of the self-segregating Anglicized set of upper India." Chaudhuri described Jawaharlal as a snob, contemptuous of those who spoke English with an Indian accent, with no understanding of contemporary Hinduism. Such criticisms are not entirely illegitimate (though at least one admirer, the Soviet author Ilya Ehrenburg, declared that for Nehru "Shakespeare did not overshadow Kalidasa, and he conversed with a Punjabi peasant as naturally as with a Cambridge professor"). But they were often sparked by animus. Those who resented Jawaharlal's near-total identification with his country challenged the authenticity of his claims to embody India. N. B. Khare, the president of the Hindu Mahasabha in 1950, described Jawaharlal Nehru as "English by education, Muslim by culture and Hindu by accident." He meant it as an insult, but in fact it was a tribute — to the eclecticism that had made Jawaharlal the finest product of the syncretic traditions to which a twentieth-century Indian was heir. Ehrenburg called Nehru "a man of great and universal culture. His interests have lain in Marxism and in the origins of religions, in Freudianism and in ethics, in the sculpture of Ellora and Elephanta, in the poetry of the English Romantics. He has discussed human discontent with Romain Rolland, revolutionary romanticism with Ernest Toller, and the destinies of Buddhism with André Malraux."

From these varied sources of inspiration emerged Nehru's most important contribution to Indian democracy — the very notion of Indianness. It is worth remembering that, amid the popular ferment that made an Italian nation out of a mosaic of principalities and statelets, the Italian nationalist Massimo Taparelli d'Azeglio had memorably written, "We have created Italy. Now all we need to do is to create Italians." Nehru never succumbed to the temptation to express a similar thought, because he believed in the existence of India and Indians for millennia before he gave words to their longings. He would never have spoken of "creating" India or Indians, merely of being the agent for the reassertion of what had always existed but had been long suppressed. Nonetheless, the India that was born in 1947 was in a very real sense a new creation: a state that made fellow citizens of the Ladakhi and the Laccadivian for the first time, that divided Punjabi from Punjabi for the first time, that asked the Keralite peasant to feel allegiance to a Kashmiri pandit ruling in Delhi, also for the first time. Nehru would not have written of the challenge of "creating" Indians, but creating Indians was what, in fact, the nationalist movement did. And Nehru it was, above all else, who welded that India into a plausible nation — the man who, through his writings, his speeches, his life, and his leadership, can be credited with the invention of the India we know today.

Jawaharlal always saw India as more than the sum of its contradictions. It is a country held together, he wrote in *The Discovery of India*, "by strong but invisible threads. . . . She is a myth and an idea" (he always feminized India), "a dream and a vision, and yet very real and present and pervasive." Who better than Nehru to incarnate this India, this idea, this present reality? Nehru articulated a vision of India as pluralism vindicated by history:

> India . . . was like an ancient palimpsest on which layer upon layer of thought and reverie had been inscribed, and yet no succeeding layer had completely hidden or erased what had been written previously. . . . Though outwardly there was diversity and infinite variety among our people, everywhere there was that tremendous impress of oneness, which had held all of us together for ages. . . . [India] was a world in itself, a culture and a civilization which gave shape to all things. Foreign influences poured in . . . and were absorbed.

> Disruptive tendencies gave rise immediately to an attempt to find a synthesis. Some kind of a dream of unity has occupied the mind of India since the dawn of civilization. That unity was not conceived as something imposed from outside, a standardization of externals or even of beliefs. It was something deeper and, within its fold, the widest tolerance of belief and custom was practiced and every variety acknowledged and even encouraged.

This was a vision of India that resolved the national argument about identity by simply bypassing it. Nehru argued that the unity of India was apparent from the outside: every Indian, whatever his differences from other Indians, was seen by foreigners as an Indian first, rather than as a Christian or Muslim, even though he might share his religion with those foreigners. For Nehru, the "Indian people" had a timeless quality, emerging from history and stretching on into the future. Not surprisingly, it was Nehru who insisted that the name India be retained in the Constitution, in the face of attempts by Prasad and others to rename the country Bharat, a piece of Hindu atavism that Jawaharlal accommodated by allowing both versions to be used. For he was above all a unifying figure for the newly independent country. In a 1953 article Nirad Chaudhuri considered Nehru "the indispensable link between the governing middle-classes and the sovereign people" of India, as well as "the bond between India and the world" . . . "India's representative to the great Western democracies, and I must add, their representative to India. . . . [W]hen Nehru takes an anti-

Western or neutral line[,] they feel they are being let down by one of themselves."

The "link," the "bridge," the embodiment of India, the man forever trying to accommodate and reconcile the country's various and disparate tendencies, even the notion of him as a turncoat to the West — these very terms point to the contradictions between conviction and compromise that marked Jawaharlal Nehru's life. His books reveal a Western intellect articulating an Indian heritage in the voice of the Enlightenment. (In this regard he made possible India's ability to compete in the globalized world of the twenty-first century, by infusing "Westernization" into Indianness institutionally, temperamentally, and philosophically.) Nehru defined Indian nationhood through the power of his ideas, in many ways like Thomas Jefferson in the United States, a figure to whom he bears considerable resemblance — a man of great intellect and sweeping vision, a wielder of words without parallel, high-minded and eloquent, yet in many ways blind to his own faults and those of others around him.

Syed Mahmud, who had known Jawaharlal since 1912, wrote in 1959 that Nehru "is essentially a man of the future. In his anxiety to build the future of his country in the shortest possible time, he sometimes lamentably ignores the present." Three decades later, in my own *The Great Indian Novel*, I portrayed Jawaharlal Nehru as the blind visionary Dhritarashtra, unable to see the realities around him while he fixed his gaze on distant ideals. Such a conceit was the privilege of a satirist, but as with all satire there was a kernel of truth in the portrait. And yet that faith in the future that animated Nehru's vision of India seems so much more valuable than the atavistic assertion of pride in the past that stirs pettier nationalists.

Until late into adulthood Jawaharlal felt keenly the need for, and depended upon, a strong father figure: first Motilal, then the Mahatma, both strong-willed individuals in relation to whom he shaped his own beliefs, and whose self-confident judgment guided, confirmed, or altered his own. (Even Patel briefly played this role between 1947 and 1950.) The gap between rhetoric and action, between conviction and execution, was particularly apparent in his relations with Mahatma Gandhi, with whom he frequently expressed disagreement but could never bring himself to make a definitive break. The profound certitude that there was always someone older and stronger to set him right if he strayed might help explain his lifelong tendency to affirm principles disconnected from practical consequences. During the freedom struggle, this was manifest in his frequent courting of arrest and enduring prison terms without any concrete effect on the British, his advocacy of the disastrous resignation of the Congress ministries in 1939, his leadership of the futile (and in the end counterproductive) Quit India movement in 1942; as prime minister, it lay in much that he said, on issues ranging from socialism to world peace, which had little relation to the real experience of the Indians in whose name he spoke. Indeed, the gap between the ideals he articulated and their achievement became one of the tragedies of Nehru's life, because the more people took him at his word, the more disillusioned they became — as with the Socialists, who broke with him precisely because they shared what he declared to be his beliefs but rejected what they saw were his actions.

But it would be wrong to see this talent for compromise in purely negative terms. Jawaharlal saw the task of nation-building as requiring inclusiveness and consensus; the hotheaded radicalism of his youth, when he was critical of Gokhale and later of Gandhi, gave way over time to a profound respect for consensus over conflict, idealism over ideology, and democracy over dictatorship. He told André Malraux that his greatest challenge was "creating a just state by just means." The equation of means and ends was fundamentally Gandhian, even if in other respects Nehru might have disavowed the label. His critics on both the left and the right saw his moderation as temporizing; the left attacked him for selling out to capitalism, the right for appeasing Indian Muslims and Pakistan. Ambedkar accused him of reducing the Congress Party to a dharamsala, or rest home, devoid of principle or policy, "open to all, fools and knaves, friends and foes, communists and secularists, reformers and orthodox and capitalists and anti-capitalists."

But this was what Jawaharlal believed Indian democracy required. "India," he told Malraux, "must struggle against herself." The statesman who epitomized the marriage of British political education, Muslim aesthetic refinement, and Hindu civilizational tolerance helped establish and affirm a democracy that has proved both freewheeling and enduring. Yet it now appears that one of the early strengths of Nehruvian India — the survival of the nationalist movement as a political party, the Congress Party serving as an all-embracing, all-inclusive agglomeration of all the major political tendencies in the country — turned out, with hindsight, to have undermined the evolution of a genuine multiparty system. Had the nationalist movement given birth to, say, three major parties — one right of center, one social democrat, one communist — a culture of principle might have evolved in India's political contention. Instead the survival of the eclectic Congress for decades as India's dominant party (a survival ensured by Nehru's talent for accommodation) stifled this process, and opposition to it (with a few honorable exceptions, like the pro-free-enterprise Swatantra Party between 1959 and 1974) emerged largely in the form of the assertion of identities to which the Congress was deemed not to have given full expression. Nehru sought to promote a politics based on the management of secular relationships, but not long after his death, politicians began to organize themselves, and even to create parties, around primordial identities, including the very elements Nehru abhorred, particularly caste, ethnicity, and religion.

The result is that instead of parties distinguished by political principle, Indian politics too often offers the spectacle of a choice between different group identities. And democratic politics is not always able to contain the country's undemocratic passions. Early in the twenty-first century India witnessed, in the state of Gujarat, a politicized form of sectarian bloodletting that took over a thousand (mainly Muslim) lives in scenes reminiscent of the partition killings. This occurred with a democratically elected government in office. This was not the freedom Nehru had fought for. Jawaharlal had written, in *The Discovery of India,* that India offered "the terrifying glimpses of dark corridors which seem to lead back to primeval night," though he had added, with typical optimism, "but also there is the fullness and warmth of the day about her." Nehru built India's political institutions with conviction and principle, but many of India's politicians increasingly reflect the qualities required to acquire power by the assertion of communal difference rather than the skills to wield it for the common good. Across the country, the democratic process has attracted figures who can win elections but who have barely a nodding acquaintance with ethics or principles, and are untroubled by the need for either.

So there is no denying the disillusionment with aspects of Indian democracy that afflicts middle-class India; many who ought to know better lapse disturbingly into a wistful longing for benign authoritarianism. Jawaharlal's daughter, Indira, suspended the country's democratic freedoms during a twenty-two-month "state of emergency" from 1975 to 1977, imprisoning her opponents, suspending civil rights, and censoring the press. It is a measure of the values she imbibed at her father's knee that she then called a free and fair election and lost it comprehensively.

The disconnect between father and daughter during Indira's formative years had a lasting impact. Indira spent the last fourteen years of her father's life by his side, in his home, serving as his official hostess and political colleague; but she failed to become his true political heir.

She had none of his intellectual gifts and few of his ideals. From his years of suffering and resistance, and even from the inspiring correspondence he addressed to her, she learned little, except for a heightened sense of her family's sacrifices, intensified by the insecurities that haunted her lonely childhood. Instead, Indira's education would always be empirical. Her proximity to Jawaharlal came when he was in office, the unquestioned leader of India and of the Third World. From this experience she imbibed a taste for power and its acquisition, with little of the sense of the larger good for which it could be used. Jawaharlal, ever the democrat, did little to prepare his daughter for high office; when this was thrust upon her, two years after his death, by Congress Party bosses hoping to capitalize on her name and pedigree, she seized the mantle of Nehruvianism but never understood its spirit. That the Jawaharlal who had warned of the temptations of dictatorship should produce a daughter who would, albeit briefly and unsuccessfully, suspend India's democracy, remains one of the great ironies of his legacy.

But it is startling to realize how the emergency is remembered in many middle-class homes as a time of order and relative honesty in government, when officials came to work and did not ask for bribes, when the streets were free of agitations and demonstrations, and blackmarketeers and hoarders were locked up along with troublesome politicians. Tyranny always serves the interests of those who are themselves untouched by it, which is why autocrats and dictators everywhere have always enjoyed some popular support. Nehru's ashes are no doubt churning the waters of his beloved Ganga at the news of public opinion polls in which a majority of India's urban middle class say that the problems of the country can best be tackled through dictatorship. Democracy, in their minds, was associated with inefficiency, corruption, and mediocrity.

But if the Nehruvian vision of democracy seems discredited, the democratic system itself has survived. Amid India's myriad problems, it is democracy that has given Indians of every imaginable caste, creed, culture, and cause the chance to break free of their lot. There is social oppression and caste tyranny, particularly in rural India, but Indian democracy offers the victims a means of redemption through the ballot box. Elections have increasingly given real political power to the lowest of India's low. For that, we must be eternally grateful to Nehru.

A related distinctive feature of the Nehruvian legacy was secularism — his visionary rejection of India's assorted bigotries and particularisms. Nehru was, by upbringing and conviction, completely secular. "I have no patience left with the legitimate and illegitimate offspring of religion," Jawaharlal wrote in a letter to his Muslim friend Syed Mahmud in 1927. He was scathing about the superstitions and petty prohibitions that came with religious observance. In a speech to students in Bombay on May 20, 1928, Nehru declared: "Much is said about the superiority of our religion, art, music and philosophy. But what are they today? Your religion has become a thing of the kitchen, as to what you can eat, and what you cannot eat, as to whom you can touch, and whom you cannot touch." Well before partition,

Jawaharlal was conscious of the danger that "religion in India will kill that country and its peoples if it is not subdued." After partition, his uncompromising commitment to Indian secularism made him the symbol of security for India's Muslims and other minorities, the assurance that pluralist India would never be reduced to Hindu India.

Nehru's distaste for religion in public life was matched by his family's disregard for it in their private lives. Displaced Kashmiris to begin with, the Nehru family tree sports Parsi, Sikh, Italian, and now Indian Christian branches, and its roots are universally seen as uncontaminated by the communal and sectarian prejudices of the Hindi-speaking cowbelt. The one strand of political opinion Nehru and his offspring abhorred was that of Hindu religious revivalism. "The [real] danger to India," Nehru declared bluntly the year before his death, "is Hindu right-wing communalism." Nehru himself was an avowed agnostic, as was his daughter until she discovered the electoral advantages of public piety. All four generations of Nehrus in public life remained secular in outlook and conduct. Their appeal transcended caste, region, and religion, something almost impossible to say of any other leading Indian politician during Nehru's life or afterward.

There could be no starker indication of the end of Nehruvianism that, fifty-five years after partition and independence, religion has again become a key determinant of political identity in India. Yet it can be argued that "Hindutva"[10] has become a credible political move-

[10]See note on Indian Political Parties and Movements, pp. xvi–xvii.

ment precisely because of the nature of the strategy pursued by the Indian state since independence in relation to its religious communities. Nehru's ostensibly secular Indian state granted major concessions to its minority religions, organized not just as religions but as social communities. Personal law, on matters concerning worship, marriage, inheritance, and divorce, was left to the religious leaders of each community to maintain and interpret; the state passed no law to alter or abridge Muslim personal law, even though Parliament, through the Hindu Code Bill, radically transformed Hindu society in these areas as early as 1956. Educational and cultural institutions of religious minorities are subsidized (in some cases almost entirely funded) by state grants; these include even explicitly religious schools. Muslim divines and preachers routinely receive government grants, and the government disburses considerable sums annually on arranging for them to travel on the annual Haj pilgrimage to Mecca. Indeed, despite the fact that a political party organized on religious lines had partitioned the country, the government did nothing to discourage political mobilization on the basis of religion, so that the rump of Jinnah's Muslim League not only continued to be active in independent India, but even became an electoral ally of the Congress Party (in Kerala).

If Muslim politicians developed a vested interest in minorityhood, the Nehruvian state evolved a vested interest in its perpetuation: support the leaders of the minority, preempt their radicalization by giving them no cause to fear the state, and so co-opt them into the national consensus. When objections to national policy were voiced on religious grounds, as over the Shah Banu affair in 1986, when a Supreme Court ruling granted a Muslim woman alimony in defiance of Muslim personal law, the state (under Nehru's grandson, Rajiv Gandhi) rushed to appease the most conservative elements in the minority community. This was not particularly secular in any sense of the term, let alone Jawaharlal Nehru's, but secularism is what Indians have called it for over five decades.

Perhaps inevitably, the Indian state constructed by Nehru came to be seen by many Hindus as an instrument to control and rein them in, while perpetuating the self-assertion of the minorities (and by this is almost always meant one particular minority, the Muslims). The "Hindutva" project so assiduously being promoted these days depends on a fundamental rejection of what Nehru stood for, by suggesting that it speaks for a true national ethos that he denied. It rejects the pluralist Indianness of *The Discovery of India* for a narrow "Hinduness." Both sides of the argument seek vindication for their views in their differing readings of Indian civilizational history, but on the cusp of the twenty-first century it was the non-Nehruvian view that did better at the ballot box.

So it is sadly true that the workings of Nehru's democratic system, which remains the best guarantee of Indian pluralism, have served to create and perpetuate India's various particularisms. The Hindu-Muslim divide is merely the most visible, but that within Hinduism, between caste Hindus and the former "Untouchables," and between the upper castes and the lower intermediate castes known as the "backwards," is actually transforming Indian society in ways that Nehru did not anticipate.

Caste, which Nehru abhorred and believed would disappear from the social matrix of modern India, has not merely survived and thrived, but has become an instrument for political mobilization.

Independent India's determination to compensate for millennia of injustice to its social underclasses meant that, from the very first, the "Scheduled Castes and Tribes" (so called because the eligible groups of Dalits and aboriginals were listed in a schedule annexed to the Constitution) were granted guaranteed quotas in schools and colleges, in government jobs, both in officialdom and in the public-sector industries, and, uniquely, in Parliament. Indeed, so complete was the country's acceptance of the principle of affirmative action that the clamor to join the bandwagon of reservations grew, and led to more and more groups wanting reservations of their own. The addition of the "backward classes" as recommended by the Mandal Commission has now taken the total of reserved jobs in the federal government and national governmental institutions to 49.5 percent, and in several states the local reservations are even higher, extending to some 69 percent in Tamil Nadu state. Despite these constitutional protections, inequalities persist between the upper castes and the former "Untouchables." Affirmative action, perhaps inevitably, benefited a minority of Dalits who were in a position to take advantage of it; independent India has witnessed the creation of privileged sections within formerly underprivileged groups, as the sons and daughters of rich and influential Scheduled Caste leaders get ahead on the strength of their caste affiliation. Caste Hindus have increasingly come to resent the offspring of cabinet ministers, for instance, benefiting from reservations and lower entry thresholds into university and government that were designed to compensate for disadvantages these scions of privilege have never personally experienced.

This has been augmented by the increasing importance of caste as a factor in the mobilization of votes. Nehru scorned the practice, though some of his aides were not above exploiting caste-based vote banks, but today candidates are picked by their parties principally with an eye to the caste loyalties they can call upon; often their appeal is overtly to voters of their own caste or subcaste, urging them to elect one of their own. The result has been a phenomenon Nehru would never have imagined, and which yet seems inevitable: the growth of caste-consciousness and casteism throughout Indian society. An uncle of mine by marriage, who was born just before independence, put it ironically to me not long ago: "In my grandparents' time, caste governed their lives: they ate, socialized, married, *lived*, according to caste rules. In my parents' time, during the nationalist movement, they were encouraged by Gandhi and Nehru to reject caste; we dropped our caste-derived surnames and declared caste a social evil. As a result, when I grew up, I was unaware of caste; it was an irrelevance at school, at work, in my social contacts; the last thing I thought about was the caste of someone I met. Now, in my children's generation, the wheel has come full circle. Caste is all-important again. Your caste determines your opportunities, your prospects, your promotions. You can't go forward unless you're a Backward." Caste politics as it is practiced in India today is the very antithesis of the political legacy Nehru had hoped to leave.

This damaging consequence of well-intentioned social and political engineering means that, in the five decades since independence, India has failed to create a single Indian community of the kind Nehru spoke about. Instead, there is greater consciousness than ever of what divides us: religion, region, caste, language, ethnicity. The Indian political system has become looser and more fragmented. Politicians mobilize support on ever-narrower lines of caste, subcaste, region, and religion. In terms of political identity, it has become more important to be a "backward caste" Yadav, a "tribal" Bodo, or a sectarian Muslim than to be an Indian. And every group claimed a larger share of a national economic pie that had long since stopped growing.

The modest size of that economic pie was itself a Nehruvian legacy. Other countries put authoritarian political structures in place to drive economic growth; in some cases, notably in Southeast Asia, this worked, and political liberalization has only slowly begun to follow in the wake of prosperity. Nehru recognized from the start that prosperity without democracy would be untenable; for him the central challenge in a pluralist society was to order national affairs to give everyone an even break, rather than to break even. In the process, Nehru's India put the political cart before the economic horse, shackling it to statist controls that emphasized distributive justice above economic growth, and discouraged free enterprise and foreign investment. The reasons for this were embedded in the Indian freedom struggle: since the

British had come to trade and stayed on to rule, Nehruvian nationalists were deeply suspicious of foreigners approaching them for commercial motives.

Nehru, like many Third World nationalists, saw the imperialism that had subjugated his people as the logical extension of international capitalism, for which he therefore felt a deep mistrust. As an idealist profoundly moved by the poverty and suffering of the vast majority of his countrymen under colonial capitalism, Nehru was attracted to noncapitalist solutions for their problems. The ideas of Fabian Socialism captured an entire generation of English-educated Indians; Nehru was no exception. As a democrat, he saw the economic well-being of the poor as indispensable for their political empowerment, and he could not entrust its attainment to the rich. In addition, the seeming success of the Soviet model — which Nehru admired for bringing about the industrialization and modernization of a large, feudal, and backward multinational state not unlike his own — appeared to offer a valuable example for India. Like many others of his generation, Nehru thought that central planning, state control of the "commanding heights" of the economy, and government-directed development were the "scientific" and "rational" means of creating social prosperity and ensuring its equitable distribution.

Self-sufficiency and self-reliance thus became the twin mantras: the prospect of allowing a Western corporation into India to "exploit" its resources immediately revived memories of British oppression. (It is ironic that in the West, freedom is associated axiomatically with capitalism, whereas in the postcolonial world freedom was seen as freedom *from* the depredations of foreign capital.) "Self-reliance" thus became a slogan and a watchword: it guaranteed both political freedom and freedom from economic exploitation. The result was a state that ensured political freedom but presided over economic stagnation; that regulated entrepreneurial activity through a system of licenses, permits, and quotas that promoted both corruption and inefficiency but did little to promote growth; that enshrined bureaucratic power at the expense of individual enterprise. For most of the first five decades since independence, India pursued an economic policy of subsidizing unproductivity, regulating stagnation, and distributing poverty. Nehru called this socialism.

The logic behind this approach, and for the dominance of the public sector, was a compound of nationalism and idealism: the conviction that items vital for the economic well-being of Indians must remain in Indian hands — not the hands of Indians seeking to profit from such activity, but the disinterested hands of the state, the father-and-mother to all Indians. It was sustained by the assumption that the public sector was a good in itself; that, even if it was not efficient or productive or competitive, it employed large numbers of Indians, gave them a stake in worshipping at Nehru's "new temples of modern India," and kept the country free from the depredations of profit-oriented capitalists who would enslave the country in the process of selling it what it needed. In this kind of thinking, performance was not a relevant criterion for judging the utility of the public sector: its inefficiencies were masked by generous subsidies from the national exchequer, and a combination of vested interests — socialist ideologues, bureaucratic management, self-protective trade unions, and captive markets — kept it beyond political criticism.

But since the public sector was involved in economic activity, it was difficult for it to be entirely exempt from economic yardsticks. Yet most of Nehru's public-sector companies made losses, draining away the Indian taxpayers' money. Several of the state-owned companies even today are kept running merely to provide jobs — or, less positively, to prevent the "social costs" (job losses, poverty, political fallout) that would result from closing them down. All this we owe to Nehru. Since economic self-sufficiency was seen by the Nehruvians as the only possible guarantee of political independence, extreme protectionism was imposed: high tariff barriers (import duties of 350 percent were not uncommon, and the top rate as recently as 1991 was 300 percent), severe restrictions on the entry of foreign goods, capital, and technology, and great pride in the manufacture within India of goods that were obsolete, inefficient, and shoddy but recognizably Indian (like the clunky Ambassador car, a revamped 1948 Morris Oxford produced by a Birla quasi monopoly, which had a steering mechanism with the subtlety of an oxcart, which guzzled gasoline like a sheikh and would shake like a guzzler, and yet enjoyed waiting lists of several years at all the dealers).

The mantra of self-sufficiency might have made some sense if, behind these protectionist walls, Indian business had been encouraged to thrive. Despite the difficulties placed in their way by the British Raj, Indian corporate houses like those of the Birlas, Tatas, and Kirloskars had built impressive business establishments by the time of independence, and could conceivably have taken on the world. Instead they found themselves being hobbled by regulations and restrictions, inspired by Nehru's socialist mistrust of the profit motive, on every conceivable aspect of economic activity: whether they could invest in a new product or a new capacity, where they could invest, how many people they could hire, whether they could fire them, what sort of expansion or diversification they could undertake, where they could sell and for how much. Initiative was stifled, government permission was mandatory before any expansion or diversification, and a mind-boggling array of permits and licenses were required before the slightest new undertaking. It is sadly impossible to quantify the economic losses inflicted on India over decades of entrepreneurs frittering away their energies in queuing for licenses rather than manufacturing products, paying bribes instead of hiring workers, wooing politicians instead of understanding consumers, "getting things done" through bureaucrats rather than doing things for themselves. This, too, is Nehru's legacy.

The combination of internal controls and international protectionism gave India a distorted economy, underproductive and grossly inefficient, making too few goods of too low a quality at too high a price. Exports of manufactured goods grew at an annual rate of 0.1 percent until 1985; India's share of world trade fell by four-fifths. Per capita income, with a burgeoning population and a modest increase in GDP, anchored India firmly to the bottom third of the world rankings. The public sector, however, grew in size though not in production, to become the largest in the world outside the Communist bloc. Meanwhile, income disparities persisted, the poor remained mired in a poverty all the more wretched for the lack of means of escape from it in a controlled economy, the public sector sat entrenched on the "commanding heights" and looked down upon the toiling, overtaxed middle class, and only bureaucrats, politicians, and a small elite of protected businessmen flourished from the management of scarcity.

India's curse, the economist Jagdish Bhagwati once observed, was to be afflicted by brilliant economists. Nehru had a weakness for such men: people like P. C. Mahalanobis, who combined intellectual brilliance and ideological wrongheadedness in equal measure, but who was given free rein by Jawaharlal to drive India's economy into a quicksand of regulatory red tape surrounding a mirage of planning. Nearly three decades after Nehru's death and long after the rest of the developing world (led by China) had demonstrated the success of a different path, a new Congress prime minister, P. V. Narasimha Rao, launched the country on economic reforms. In place of the Nehruvian mantra of self-sufficiency, India was to become more closely integrated into the world economic system. This repudiation of Nehruvianism has survived and become part of the new conventional wisdom. Though there is no doubt that economic reform faces serious political obstacles in democratic India, and change is often made with the hesitancy of governments looking over their electoral shoulders, there is now a definitive rupture of the Nehruvian link between democracy and socialism: one is no longer the corollary of the other. The bogey of the East India Company has finally been laid to rest.

And yet there is no denying one vital legacy of Nehru's economic planning — the creation of an infrastructure for excellence in science and technology, which has become a source of great self-confidence and competitive advantage for the country today. Nehru was always fascinated by science and scientists; he made it a point to attend the annual Indian Science Congress every year, and he gave free rein (and taxpayers' money) to scientists in whom he had confidence to build high-quality institutions. Men like Homi Bhabha and Vikram Sarabhai constructed the platform for Indian accomplishments in the fields of atomic energy and space research; they and their successors have given the country a scientific establishment without peer in the developing world. Jawaharlal's establishment of the Indian Institutes of Technology (and the spur they provided to other lesser institutions) have produced many of the finest minds in Silicon Valley; today, an IIT degree is held in the same reverence in the U.S. as one from MIT or Caltech, and India's extraordinary leadership in the software industry is the indirect result of Jawaharlal Nehru's faith in scientific education.

Of course this record also masks much mediocrity; overbureaucratized and underfunded scientific institutes that prompted gifted researchers like Har Gobind Khurana and Subramanyam Chandrasekhar to take their talents abroad and win Nobel Prizes for the U.S. rather than India. It is striking that post-independence India has not replicated, at any of Nehru's much-vaunted scientific institutions, the success of pre-independence scientists like C. V. Raman, Satyen Bose, or Meghnad Saha, who had left their marks on the world of physics in the first thirty years of the twentieth century with the Raman effect, the Bose-Einstein statistics, and the Saha equation. Still, Nehru left India with the world's second-largest pool of trained scientists and engineers, integrated into the global intellectual system, to a degree without parallel outside the developed West.

Nehru was skeptical of Western claims to stand for freedom and democracy when India's historical experience of colonial oppression and exploitation appeared to bear out the opposite. His conclusion was to see a moral equivalence between the two rival power blocs in the cold war, a position that led to nonalignment. Nehru saw this as the only possible stance compatible with the self-respect of a newly independent nation, and one which entitled India to take an independent position on each international issue. The limitations of his approach became apparent near the end of his own life, and today the end of the cold war has left India without a global conflict to be nonaligned against. Nonalignment, its defenders suggested, gave credibility to Indian nationalism by providing it with an overarching international purpose; without it, some questioned whether the idea of India could have stood its ground. But the point about the nationalist idea in India was that, for all the Nehruvian rhetoric, it was not dependent on an internationalist mission: its principal relevance was internal, in "creating Indians" out of the world's most disparate collection of fellow citizens. Today one might argue that the changes in India's external orientation necessitated by its economic reforms and by the emergence of the United States as the sole superpower have made nonalignment a rhetorical device at best, an irrelevance at worst. Be that as it may, the point remains that nonalignment is no longer a sufficient explanation for India's interests on the world stage. Once again, Nehruvianism is passé.

A retired Indian diplomat, Badruddin Tyabji, surveying the conduct of Nehru's foreign policy after Nehru's death, lamented sardonically:

> Subjectivity still rules the roost, though the great Subject himself died in 1964. His successors now quibble over the contents of his "system," though he had no system. He had only behaved like himself, and no one can do that any more for him.

The political ethos Nehru promoted was one of staunch anti-imperialism, a determination to safeguard India against foreign domination and internal division, and a commitment — at least in principle — to the uplift of the poorest sections of Indian society. These concerns fused together in the four pillars of Nehruvianism. If they were infused by what sometimes seemed excessively idealist rhetoric, Jawaharlal had a typical retort: "idealism," he declared, "is the realism of tomorrow." Tomorrow, however, has a habit of finding its own realisms. The last Congress Party government of Prime Minister Narasimha Rao paid little but lip service to the traditional leitmotivs of the Nehru legacy. Instead, Rao tried to manage the contradictory pulls of India's various particularist tendencies by seeking to accommodate them in a new consensus: economic reforms to invite foreign investment, to reduce the government's power to command the economy, and to spur growth, coupled with politics that gave a little to each new group demand. The governments that have followed his have gone even further, even beginning to dismantle the public sector that was among Nehru's proudest creations.

And yet there can be no greater measure of the extent to which Jawaharlal Nehru dominated the political, intellectual, and moral ethos of his day than the tribute paid to him by his great critic Atal Behari Vajpayee, the opposition leader who would one day succeed Nehru both as foreign minister (in 1977) and as prime minister (in 1996). Upon Jawaharlal's death, Vajpayee declared in Parliament that "a dream has remained half-fulfilled, a song has become silent, and a flame has vanished into the Unknown. The dream was of a world free of fear and hunger; the song a great epic resonant with the spirit of the Gita and as fragrant as a rose; the flame a candle which burnt all night long, showing us the way." He added that Nehru was "the orchestrator of the impossible and inconceivable," one who "was not afraid of compromise but would never compromise under duress." Vajpayee went on to mourn "that vibrancy and independence of mind, that quality of being able to befriend the opponent and enemy, that gentlemanliness, that greatness" that marked Nehru. When he took over as minister of external affairs in India's first non-Congress government in 1977, Vajpayee noticed that a portrait of Nehru was missing from its usual spot in the ministerial chamber, removed in an excess of zeal by functionaries anxious to please the new rulers. The lifelong critic of the Congress demanded its return. As he had said in his elegy, "the sun has set, yet by the shadow of the stars we must find our way."

So one must never forget the man himself, and his stamp on the age. His most comprehensive biographer, the late Gopal, put it best:

> No one who lived in India during the enchantment of the Nehru years needs to be reminded of the positive, generous spirit, the quality of style, the fresh and impulsive curiosity, the brief flares of temper followed by gentle contrition and the engaging streak of playfulness, all of which went along with an unrelenting sense of duty, a response to large issues, an exercise of reason and unaffiliated intelligence in human affairs, an intense, but not exclusive, patriotism and, above all, complete and transparent personal integrity. . . . To a whole generation of Indians he was not so much a leader as a companion who expressed and made clearer a particular view of the present and a vision of the future. The combination of intellectual and moral authority was unique in his time.

The Indian novelist Raja Rao once spoke of the "secret historicity" of Jawaharlal's mere presence. The American statesman Adlai Stevenson, introducing Nehru to a Chicago audience in 1949, observed:

> We live in an age swept by tides of history so powerful they shatter human understanding. Only a tiny handful of men have influenced the implacable forces of our time. To this small company of the

> truly great, Pandit Jawaharlal Nehru belongs. . . . He belongs to the even smaller company of historic figures who wore a halo in their own lifetimes.

Nehru, Singapore's Lee Kuan Yew wrote, "had to stand the test of two judgments: first, how well he succeeded in overthrowing the old order and second, whether he has succeeded in establishing a new order which is better than the old." Lee's cautious verdict was that "nobody can say that his reputation has been tarnished as a result of attaining power." Nehru's idea of India has held, though his legacy to India remains a mixed one. Of the four major pillars of his system, two — democratic institution-building and staunch secularism — were indispensable to the country's survival as a pluralist land; a third, nonalignment, preserved its self-respect and enhanced its international standing without bringing any concrete benefits to the Indian people; the fourth, socialist economics, was disastrous, condemning the Indian people to poverty and stagnation and engendering inefficiency, red-tapism, and corruption on a scale rarely rivaled elsewhere. In some ways, Jawaharlal seems curiously dated, a relic of another era; in others, such as in the development of India's technological, nuclear, and satellite programs, a vindicated visionary. He called the dams and factories he built the "new temples" of modern India, but failed to realize the hold the old temples would continue to have on the Indian imagination. He created the technological institutes that have positioned India for leadership in the computer age, but he did not understand that software and spirituality could go hand in hand, that India in the twenty-first century would be a land of both programming and prayers. Nearly four decades after Nehru's death, the consensus he constructed has frayed: democracy endures, secularism is besieged, nonalignment is all but forgotten, and socialism barely clings on.

"Progress," Jawaharlal declared toward the end of his life, "ultimately has to be measured by the quality of human beings — how they are improving, how their lot is improving, and how they are adapting themselves to modern ways and yet keep their feet firmly planted on their soil." By his own measure, India's progress has been mixed. India's challenge today is both to depart from his legacy and to build on it, to sustain an India open to the contention of ideas and interests within it, unafraid of the power or the products of the outside world, secure in a national identity that transcends its divisions, and determined to liberate and fulfill the creative energies of her people. If India succeeds, it must acknowledge that he laid the foundation for such a success; if India fails, it will find in Nehru many of the seeds of its failure.

On his desk, Jawaharlal Nehru kept two totems — a gold statuette of Mahatma Gandhi and a bronze cast of the hand of Abraham Lincoln, which he would occasionally touch for comfort. The two objects reflected the range of his sources of inspiration: he often spoke of his wish to confront problems with the heart of the Mahatma and the hand of Lincoln. Nehru's time may indeed have passed; but it says something about the narrowing of the country's intellectual heritage that both objects ended up in a museum — and his heirs just kept the desk.

Who's Who: Short Biographical Notes on Personalities Mentioned

Sheikh Abdullah (1905–1982): Kashmiri leader; founded the National Conference in Kashmir state in 1938, opposing the maharajah on a secular, democratic platform as an ally of Jawaharlal Nehru and the Congress; prime minister of Kashmir, 1948–53, then arrested and imprisoned; chief minister of Kashmir, 1975–82

Maulana Muhammad Ali (1878–1931): nationalist Muslim; leader of Khilafat agitation; president of the Congress, 1923

Dr. B. R. Ambedkar (1891–1956): leader of the Harijans (formerly "Untouchables," now called Dalits); leading framer of India's Constitution; law minister, 1947–51

Maulana Abul Kalam Azad (1888–1958): Muslim scholar and Indian nationalist leader; president of the Congress, 1923, and again, 1940–46; devoted much of his political life to promoting Hindu-Muslim unity and seeking to prevent the partition of India; minister for education, 1947–58

Annie Besant (1847–1933): British-born "Indian" nationalist and theosophist; started Indian Home Rule League; president of the Congress, 1917

Ghanshyam Das (G. D.) Birla (1894–1992): Indian industrialist; supporter and frequent host of Mahatma Gandhi

Subhas Chandra Bose (1897–1945): Indian nationalist hero, known as "Netaji," or "Respected Leader"; resigned from the Indian Civil Service in 1921 to oppose British rule; president of the Congress, 1938–39; escaped British internment to travel to Germany in 1941; organized the Indian National Army to fight the British in Burma; died at war's end in crash of a Japanese airplane

Sir Stafford Cripps (1889–1952): British Labour Party leader and government negotiator on Indian affairs; solicitor-general, 1930–31; ambassador to the USSR, 1940–42; minister of aircraft production, 1942–45; president of the Board of Trade, 1945–47; chancellor of the Exchequer, 1947–50; led two unsuccessful missions to India to discuss the country's constitutional future

Chitta Ranjan (C. R.) Das (1870–1925): leading Calcutta lawyer who cofounded the Swaraj Party within the Congress in 1922; president of the Congress, 1922

Feroze Gandhi (1912–1960): Congress Party volunteer and aide of Kamala Nehru; married Jawaharlal's daughter, Indira, 1942; member of Parliament, 1951–60

Indira Nehru Gandhi (1917–1984): daughter of Jawaharlal Nehru and his official hostess after 1947; president of the Congress Party, 1959; minister of information and broadcasting in Prime Minister Shastri's cabinet, 1964–66; prime minister of India, 1966–77 and 1980–84; declared state of emergency and arrested political opponents, 1975–77

Mahatma Gandhi (1869–1948): "Father of the Nation"; India's preeminent nationalist leader; devised philosophy of nonviolent resistance embodied in satyagraha; served as political and spiritual guide of the Congress while refusing to accept office himself; insisted means and ends had to be equally just; sought to calm the fires of communal violence; assassinated by a Hindu fanatic shortly after independence

Gopal Krishna Gokhale (1866–1915): leading Indian "Moderate" nationalist; teacher and social reformer who founded the Servants of India Society in 1905; president of the Congress, 1905; admired by Mahatma Gandhi for his reasoned and temperate advocacy of India's freedom

Sir Mohamed Iqbal (1876–1938): highly respected philosopher and poet in Persian and Urdu; author of nationalist song "Sare Jahan se Achha Hindustan hamara"; later an advocate of Pakistan as a Muslim homeland within India

Lord Irwin (1881–1959): British politician; viceroy of India, 1926–31; concluded Gandhi-Irwin Pact, 1931; later, as Earl Halifax, foreign secretary, 1938–40, and British ambassador to the United States during World War Two, 1941–46

Mohammed Ali Jinnah (1876–1948): father and "Qaid-e-Azam" of Pakistan; president of the Muslim League, 1916, 1920, 1934–48; leading advocate of Congress-League cooperation and Hindu-Muslim unity who later began to advocate the partition of the country; governor-general of Pakistan, 1947–48

Chaudhuri Khaliquzzaman (1889–1973): close friend and contemporary of Jawaharlal Nehru and leading member of the Congress until 1937, when he joined the Muslim League; migrated to Pakistan upon partition

Khan Abdul Ghaffar Khan (1891–1991): the "Frontier Gandhi"; Congress leader of the North-West Frontier Province, organized nonviolent resistance group called the Khudai Khidmatgars; opposed partition and was repeatedly jailed for long periods by the government of Pakistan

Liaquat Ali Khan (1895–1951): leader of the Muslim League and its general secretary, 1936–47; minister of finance in India's interim government, 1946–47; prime minister of Pakistan, 1947–51; assassinated by an Afghan Muslim gunman

Sir Sikandar Hyat Khan (1892–1942): secular Muslim statesman; deputy governor of the Reserve Bank of India, 1935–37; leader of the Unionist Party and chief minister of Punjab, 1937–42

Rafi Ahmed Kidwai (1894–1954): close friend and political associate of Jawaharlal from his home state, U.P.; minister in U.P., 1937–39 and 1946–47; intermittent member of Nehru's cabinet, 1947–54; resigned from the Congress Party after independence but was later reconciled

Acharya J. B. Kripalani (1888–1982): general secretary of the Congress, 1934–46; president in 1946; resigned from the Congress after independence

Lord Linlithgow (1887–1952): Second Marquis of Linlithgow and viceroy of India, 1936–43; declared war on Germany in 1939 without consulting elected Indian leaders, thereby triggering resignation of Congress ministries in the provinces

Syed Mahmud (1889–1971): friend and contemporary of Jawaharlal's at Cambridge; close associate, including as Congress minister in Bihar, 1937–39 and 1946–52

K. D. Malaviya (1904–1981): Allahabad lawyer and Congress activist

V. K. Krishna Menon (1896–1974): Indian nationalist; secretary of the India League in London, 1929–47; Indian high commissioner in London, 1947–52; led Indian delegations to the United Nations throughout the 1950s; member of Nehru cabinet, 1956–62, including as minister of defense, 1957–62

Edwina Mountbatten (1901–1960): British heiress who married Lord Louis Mountbatten, 1922; close friend of Jawaharlal Nehru

Lord Mountbatten of Burma (1900–1979): member of British nobility; served as Supreme Allied Commander Southeast Asia in World War Two, 1943–46; viceroy of India, March to August 1947; governor-general of India, August 1947 to June 1948; retired after further military service; assassinated by Irish Republican Army

Padmaja Naidu (1900–1975): daughter of Sarojini Naidu and close friend of Jawaharlal; governor of West Bengal, 1969–70

Sarojini Naidu (1879–1949): nationalist, poet, and feminist; as India's leading woman poet, was dubbed the "Nightingale of India"; close associate of Mahatma Gandhi and Jawaharlal Nehru; first Indian woman to become president of the Congress, 1925; governor of Uttar Pradesh, 1947–49

Jayaprakash Narayan (1902–1979): leading Congress socialist; broke with Jawaharlal Nehru after independence and led the Socialist Party; inspired a movement for "Total Revolution" in 1974–75 that led Indira Gandhi to declare a state of emergency

Kamala Kaul Nehru (1899–1936): wife of Jawaharlal, whom she married in 1916, mother of Indira, and mentor of Feroze Gandhi; died of tuberculosis at age thirty-six

Motilal Nehru (1861–1931): father of Jawaharlal; leading Allahabad lawyer; president of the Congress, 1919 and 1928; cofounded (with C. R. Das) the Swaraj Party within the Congress and led it in the Central Assembly, 1924–26

Bipin Chandra Pal (1858–1932): "Extremist" leader of the Congress; editor of Motilal Nehru's newspaper the *Independent*; resigned from the Congress after disagreeing with Gandhi's approach

Ranjit Pandit (1893–1944): brother-in-law of Jawaharlal Nehru; married Vijayalakshmi ("Nan") Nehru in 1921; imprisoned for participation in noncooperation movement; jail companion of Jawaharlal

Vijayalakshmi Pandit (1900–1990): sister of Jawaharlal Nehru, known as "Nan"; married Ranjit Pandit in 1921; Congress activist, minister in U.P. government, 1937–39 and 1946; ambassador to the USSR, 1947–49, and to the

USA, 1949–51; first woman president of the United Nations General Assembly, 1953–54; high commissioner to Britain, 1954–61; governor of Maharashtra, 1962–64; in later years, fierce critic of her niece, Prime Minister Indira Gandhi

Sardar Vallabhbhai Patel (1875–1950): close associate of Mahatma Gandhi from his earliest political campaigns and elder statesman of the Congress Party under Jawaharlal; formidable administrator and organizer of conservative leanings; president of the Congress, 1931; as deputy prime minister and home minister, 1947–50, organized and led the integration of the princely states into the Indian Union and consolidated the new state

Rajendra Prasad (1884–1963): early supporter of Mahatma Gandhi and associate of Patel; president of the Congress, 1934, 1939, and 1947–48; president of the Constituent Assembly, 1946–50; first president of the Republic of India, 1950–62

Lala Lajpat Rai (1865–1928): leading "Extremist" Congressman, known as the "Lion of the Punjab"; president of the Congress, 1920; died of injuries inflicted by police during nationalist demonstration against Simon Commission, 1928

C. Rajagopalachari (1878–1972): early supporter of Gandhian noncooperation and leading member of the Congress who never held the presidency; chief minister of Madras, 1937–39 and 1952–54; disagreed with Quit

India movement and resigned from the Congress, 1942, but rejoined, 1946; governor of West Bengal, 1947–48; governor-general of India, 1948–50; cabinet minister, 1950–51; resigned from the Congress in protest against Jawaharlal Nehru's policies and founded conservative Swatantra Party, 1959

Sir Tej Bahadur Sapru (1875–1949): Liberal Party leader; law member of the Viceroy's Council, 1920–23

Sardar Baldev Singh (1902–1961): Sikh leader in the Punjab; member of the interim government, 1946–47; minister of defense, 1947–52

Purushottam Das Tandon (1882–1962): conservative Congress leader of Hindu traditionalist leanings; candidate for mayor of Allahabad, 1923, but supplanted by Jawaharlal Nehru because of his unacceptability to Muslims; elected president of the Congress, 1950, but forced to resign because of differences with Jawaharlal

Bal Gangadhar Tilak (1856–1920): major Indian nationalist figure and leader of the "Extremists"; lecturer and journalist in Poona, edited newspapers in both English and Marathi; sentenced to long periods of imprisonment by the British; author of scholarly works in history and philosophy

Atal Behari Vajpayee (1924–): leader of the Bharatiya Jana Sangh (now Bharatiya Janata Party) and skilled parliamentarian; minister of external affairs in Janata

Party government, 1977–79; prime minister of India, 1996 and 1998–present

Lord Wavell (1883–1950): British general, commander in chief of British forces in the Middle East, 1939–41, and in India, 1941–43; viceroy of India, 1943–47

Lord Willingdon (1866–1941): British colonial administrator; governor of Bombay, 1913–19, and of Madras, 1919–24; governor-general of Canada, 1926–31; viceroy of India, 1931–36

A Note on Sources

As stated in the Preface, this book has involved no original research into the archives; it is a reinterpretation of material largely in the public domain. The extensive quotes from Jawaharlal Nehru are all from his own published writings (and in a few cases from newspaper accounts of his statements); the volumes I have consulted are listed in the Select Bibliography that follows. I have delved into several biographies, the most useful of which I found to be Sarvepalli Gopal's magisterial three-volume study and M. J. Akbar's highly readable work, both of which wear their political points of view on their sleeves. The textual references to both men, and to the more disappointing effort of Stanley Wolpert, relate to their biographies listed in the Bibliography. The text also cites such writers as André Malraux, Norman Cousins, and the Indian diplomat Badruddin Tyabji; once again the corresponding books may be found in the Bibliography. Rafiq Zakaria's 1959 anthology and K. Natwar Singh's recent compilation of tributes expressed by a wide range of world figures shortly after Nehru's death is the source of many of the quotations in chapters 9 and 10.

I was privileged to have several conversations with Phillips Talbot, who first met Nehru as a visiting student in 1939 and over the next twenty-five years as journalist, scholar, and diplomat, and the quotations from him are from these conversations, not from any published material. From my departure for graduate school in the United States in 1975 to his death in 1993, my late father, Chandran Tharoor, peppered me with a remarkable array of newspaper clippings on Indian politics and history, many of which I have used and quoted from. My friends Arun Kumar and Ramu Damodaran have read the manuscript with care and offered me invaluable information and insights of their own, for which I am most grateful.

It hardly needs stating that, in distilling such a wealth of material into a short volume, I have made my own selections of facts and material on which to dwell. The responsibility for any errors of detail or interpretation, and indeed of omission, are mine alone.

Select Bibliography

WORKS BY JAWAHARLAL NEHRU

Soviet Russia: Some Random Sketches and Impressions (Allahabad: Ram Mohan Lal, 1928)

Glimpses of World History (Allahabad: Kitabistan, 2 vols., 1934–35)

An Autobiography (London: John Lane, 1936)

Letters from a Father to a Daughter (Allahabad: Kitabistan, 1938)

Towards Freedom (New York: John Day, 1941)

The Discovery of India (1945; reprint, New Delhi: Nehru Memorial Fund, 1988)

A Bunch of Old Letters (New Delhi: Asia Publishing House, 1959)

India's Foreign Policy: Selected Speeches (New Delhi: Publications Division, 1961)

Selected Speeches, September 1946 to April 1961 (New Delhi: Publications Division, 1961)

Selected Works of Jawaharlal Nehru, First Series, vols. 1–15, ed. M. Chalapati Rau, H. Y. Sharada Prasad, and B. R. Nanda (New Delhi: Orient Longman, 1972)

Selected Works of Jawaharlal Nehru, Second Series, vols. 1–16, ed. S. Gopal (New Delhi: Nehru Museum and Memorial Library, 1984)

Works by Nehru Family Members

Indira Gandhi, *My Truth* (New Delhi: Vision Books, 1981)

Sonia Gandhi, ed., *Freedom's Daughter: Letters between Indira Gandhi and Jawaharlal Nehru, 1922–39* (London: Hodder and Stoughton, 1989)

Sonia Gandhi, ed., *Two Alone, Two Together: Letters between Indira Gandhi and Jawaharlal Nehru, 1940–64* (London: Hodder and Stoughton, 1992)

Krishna Nehru Hutheesing, *We Nehrus* (New York: Holt, Rinehart and Winston, 1967)

Vijayalakshmi Pandit, *The Scope of Happiness* (New York: Crown, 1979)

Biographical Works on Jawaharlal Nehru

M. J. Akbar, *Nehru: The Making of India* (London: Viking, 1988)

Bharatiya Vidya Bhavan, USA, *Jawaharlal Nehru: A Photo Perspective* (New York: Bharatiya Vidya Bhavan, 1989)

Michael Brecher, *Nehru: A Political Biography* (London: Oxford University Press, 1959)

Norman Cousins, ed., *Profiles of Nehru* (New Delhi: India Book Company, 1966)

A. K. Damodaran, *Jawaharlal Nehru: A Communicator and Democratic Leader* (New Delhi: Radiant Publishers/Nehru Memorial Museum & Library, 1997)

Michael Edwardes, *Nehru: A Political Biography* (London: Penguin, 1971)

Sarvepalli Gopal, *Jawaharlal Nehru: A Biography*

Volume One: 1889–1947 (Delhi: Oxford University Press, 1975)

Volume Two: 1947–1956 (Delhi: Oxford University Press, 1979)

Volume Three: 1956–1964 (Delhi: Oxford University Press, 1984)

H. V. Kamath, *Last Days of Jawaharlal Nehru* (Calcutta: Jayasree Prakashan, 1977)

M. O. Mathai, *Reminiscences of the Nehru Age* (Delhi: Vikas, 1978)

M. O. Mathai, *My Days with Nehru* (Delhi: Vikas, 1979)

Frank Moraes, *Jawaharlal Nehru: A Biography* (New York: Macmillan, 1956)

B. N. Mullick, *My Years with Nehru: The Chinese Betrayal* (New Delhi: Vikas, 1972)

K. Natwar Singh, ed., *The Legacy of Nehru* (New Delhi: Har-Anand, 1996)

Stanley Wolpert, *Nehru: A Tryst with Destiny* (New York: Oxford University Press, 1996)

Rafiq Zakaria, ed., *A Study of Nehru* (Bombay: Times of India, 2nd rev. ed., 1960)

Other Works

M. J. Akbar, *Kashmir: Behind the Vale* (New Delhi: Viking, 1991)

A. Appadorai, *Essays in Indian Politics and Foreign Policy* (Delhi: Vikas, 1971)

Maulana Abul Kalam Azad, *India Wins Freedom* (Hyderabad: Orient Longman, 1988)

J. Bandyopadhyaya, *The Making of India's Foreign Policy* (Calcutta: Allied, 1970)

Krishan Bhatia, *The Ordeal of Nationhood* (New York: Atheneum, 1971)

Catherine Clément, *Nehru and Edwina* (New Delhi: Penguin, 1996)

Larry Collins and Dominique Lapierre, *Mountbatten and Independent India* (Delhi: Vikas, 1982)

Reginald Coupland, *The Constitutional Problem in India* (London: Oxford University Press, 1944)

J. P. Dalvi, *Himalayan Blunder* (Bombay: Thacker, 1969)

C. Dasgupta, *War and Diplomacy in Kashmir 1947–48* (New Delhi: Sage Publications, 2002)

Michael Edwardes, "Illusion and Reality in India's Foreign Policy," *International Affairs* 41 (January 1965)

Katherine Frank, *Indira* (Boston: Houghton Mifflin, 2002)

John Kenneth Galbraith, *Ambassador's Journal* (Boston: Houghton Mifflin, 1969)

Ramachandra Guha, "Democracy's Biggest Gamble," *World Policy Journal* (Spring 2002)

Ramachandra Guha, "Nirad Chaudhuri's Nehru," *The Hindu Magazine*, November 24, 2002

Y. D. Gundevia, *Outside the Archives* (Hyderabad: Orient Longman, 1984)

Welles Hangen, *After Nehru, Who?* (London: Rupert Hart-Davis, 1963)
Selig S. Harrison, *India: The Most Dangerous Decade* (Madras: Oxford University Press, 1960)
H. V. Hodson, *The Great Divide* (London: Hutchinson, 1969)
Prem Shankar Jha, *Kashmir 1947* (Delhi: Oxford University Press, 1996)
B. M. Kaul, *The Untold Story* (Bombay: Jaico, 1969)
Sunil Khilani, *The Idea of India* (New Delhi: Viking Penguin, 1997)
B. Krishna, *Indian Freedom Struggle* (New Delhi: Manohar, 2002)
André Malraux, *Anti-Memoirs* (New York: Henry Holt, 1990)
Zareer Masani, *Indira Gandhi: A Biography* (New York: Thomas Y. Crowell, 1975)
Neville Maxwell, *India's China War* (London: Jonathan Cape, 1970)
Neville Maxwell, "Reconsiderations: Jawaharlal Nehru," *Foreign Affairs* 52 (April 1974)
Ved Mehta, *Portrait of India* (New York: Farrar, Straus & Giroux, 1970)
K. P. S. Menon, *Yesterday and Today* (New Delhi: Allied, 1976)
Frank Moraes, *Witness to an Era* (Delhi: Vikas, 1973)
Janet Morgan, *Edwina Mountbatten: A Life of Her Own* (New York: Scribner, 1991)
A. G. Noorani, *Our Credulity and Negligence* (Bombay: Ramdas G. Bhatkal, 1963)
D. G. Tendulkar, *Mahatma* (Bombay: Publications Division, 2nd ed., 1961)

Raj Thapar, *All These Years* (New Delhi: Seminar, 1991)

Shashi Tharoor, "E Pluribus, India," *Foreign Affairs* (January/Febuary 1998)

Shashi Tharoor, *Reasons of State* (Delhi: Vikas, 1982)

Shashi Tharoor, *India: From Midnight to the Millennium* (New York: Arcade, 1997)

Badr-ud-din Tyabji, *Indian Policies and Practice* (New Delhi: Oriental Publishers, 1972)

Lord Wavell, *Viceroy's Journal*, ed. Penderel Moon (London: Oxford University Press, 1972)

Muhammad Yunus, *Persons, Passions and Politics* (Delhi: Vikas, 1980)

Philip Ziegler, *Mountbatten* (London: Fontana/Collins, 1986)

Index